What Readers Are Saying About *Pragmatic Guide to JavaScript*

I wish I had owned this book when I first started out doing JavaScript! *Pragmatic Guide to JavaScript* will take you a big step ahead in programming real-world JavaScript by showing you what is going on behind the scenes in popular JavaScript libraries and giving you no-nonsense advice and background information on how to do the right thing. With the condensed years of experience of one of the best JavaScript developers around, it's a must-read with great reference to everyday JavaScript tasks.

► **Thomas Fuchs**
  Creator of the script.aculo.us framework

An impressive collection of very practical tips and tricks for getting the most out of JavaScript in today's browsers, with topics ranging from fundamentals such as form validation and JSON handling to application examples such as mashups and geolocation. I highly recommend this book for anyone wanting to be more productive with JavaScript in their web applications.

► **Dylan Schiemann**
  CEO at SitePen, cofounder of the Dojo Toolkit

There are a number of JavaScript books on the market today, but most of them tend to focus on the new or inexperienced JavaScript programmer. Porteneuve does no such thing, and this Pragmatic Guide is a better book for it. If you're a novice, go elsewhere first, and then when you have some scripting under your belt, come back; if you've worked with JavaScript before, then *Pragmatic Guide to JavaScript* takes a set of techniques that you may have heard about or seen and makes them useful to you. Recommended.

► **Stuart Langridge**
  kryogenix.org, @sil

Pragmatic Guide to JavaScript

Pragmatic Guide to JavaScript

Christophe Porteneuve

The Pragmatic Bookshelf
Raleigh, North Carolina   Dallas, Texas

Our Pragmatic courses, workshops, and other products can help you and your team create better software and have more fun. For more information, as well as the latest Pragmatic titles, please visit us at http://www.pragprog.com.

The team that produced this book includes:

Editor:	David McClintock
Indexing:	Potomac Indexing, LLC
Copy edit:	Kim Wimpsett
Layout:	Steve Peter
Production:	Janet Furlow
Customer support:	Ellie Callahan
International:	Juliet Benda

ISBN-10: 1-934356-67-0
ISBN-13: 978-1-934356-67-8
Printed on acid-free paper.
P1.0 printing, November 2010
Version: 2010-11-4

Contents

Dedication

Pour Élodie, ma femme, l'étoile de ma vie.

To Élodie, my wife, always my shining star.

Acknowledgments

Writing a book is never easy. A technical book doesn't need a plot and spares the author the anguish of the blank page, but it subjects the author to a world of pressure from peers and the duties to be technically accurate and to convey best practices. This is why writing a book remains a significant endeavor and why authors can use all the help they can get.

In writing this book, I am first and foremost indebted to the amazing creators of the frameworks I mention and use. Not only did they grace the world with their praiseworthy work, but many also took the time to review this book and make sure I didn't unintentionally disgrace their brainchildren. I owe heartfelt thanks to Sam Stephenson, Thomas Fuchs, John Resig, Alex Russell, Jack Slocum, and a large number of core developers and contributors who I couldn't possibly have enough space to name here. I am even more indebted to the members of the Prototype Core team. They've been a helpful, highly skilled bunch with whom I've learned so much, especially Andrew Dupont, Tobie Langel, and Juriy Zaytsev.

In the search for technical accuracy and overall book bettering, a number of people, some of whom I mentioned already, gracefully agreed to review this book and reduce the chances of my making a fool of myself. And I was indeed graced with an outstanding list of reviewers! I bow with respect and gratitude to Dion Almaer, Arnaud Berthomier, Aaron Gustafson, Christian Heilmann, Dylan Schiemann, and Sam Stephenson.

This is my second book with the Pragmatic Programmers. Once again, Dave Thomas and Andy Hunt opened their virtual doors to me and let me work with their wonderful staff on this new series of books, the Pragmatic Guides. It's been a thrill to work with the series editor, Susannah Davidson Pfalzer; my editor, David McClintock (making his Prag debut); the keen-eyed Kim Wimpsett for copyediting; the wizardly Sara Lynn Eastler for producing a Pragmatic-quality index; and the skillful Steve Peter, whose typesetting makes the book look good.

Last but by no means least, I am forever grateful to Élodie, my beloved wife. She's put up with four books over the past five years, and she's always been supportive and loving. I am the luckiest guy on Earth, and I could not dream of a better spouse. This book, once again, is for her.

Introduction

If you've been paying even minimal attention to JavaScript these past few years, you've heard this before: it's the Next Big Language. Once the province of half-baked implementations and useless scrolling messages, it has become a world-class, dynamic, object-oriented language with super-fast implementations on the client and server sides.

On the one hand, JavaScript's designers are endowing it with a new healthy dose of power, through the EcmaScript 5 (ES5) specification. On the other hand, kick-ass engines (such as V8, JavaScriptCore, SpiderMonkey, Rhino, and Carakan) and emergent standards and technologies (with CommonJS[1] and Node[2] in the lead) make it usable both in browsers and as stand-alone, powerful architectures on the server. Even the upcoming Internet Explorer 9 is upping its JavaScript game with the promise of huge speed boosts.

Not only is JavaScript a powerful, dynamic language, but it now has a rich ecosystem of professional-grade development tools, infrastructures, frameworks, and tool kits. It is versatile, fast, and very well suited to a wide range of programming tasks, especially when it comes to web-based applications and services.

It's time to dive in!

What's This Book About, and Who Is It For?

This book is not really intended to teach you "JavaScript the language." For one thing, the language itself is not very complicated, so if you have prior experience in programming any reasonably common language—even if it's just the basics (variables, loops, and so on)—you'll get your bearings easily enough. You don't need to actually know some JavaScript already (although it could help), and you certainly don't need to be any sort of programming guru.

Actually, if you're looking for the nitty-gritty and the hardcore technical details of JavaScript, you'll be better off reading a dedicated resource, such as

---

1. http://commonjs.org/
2. http://nodejs.org/

the "JavaScript core skills" section of Opera's excellent Web Standards Curriculum.[3] Should you ever need even more intricate, implementation-level details, you could then head to either the official specs of the language or one of the massive "bible" books such as David Flanagan's *JavaScript: The Definitive Guide* [Fla06].

This book aims to provide you with quick yet qualitative solutions to common client-side JavaScript-based tasks, from low-level stuff (such as getting a reference to a DOM element) to intricate features (such as Ajax-based autocompletion). This means we'll tackle JavaScript, CSS, the DOM, Ajax, JSON, and more. We won't go deep into the server side; this book is mostly on the client side of things (most often the browser). You'll encounter a couple of tiny PHP scripts along the way, for illustration purposes, but you could write your server side any way you like—including in JavaScript, for instance, with Node!

It's not just for copying and pasting, either. The text for each task takes care to highlight the key concepts, the potential gotchas, and the technical tricks you should take away from the task. Ultimately, you should step away from this book as a better JavaScript programmer.

This Book and JavaScript Libraries

Let's speak plainly here. If you're doing any sort of nontrivial JavaScript programming and you're not relying heavily on good, established frameworks for it, You're Doing It Wrong. On the browser side, effectively pulling off web page scripting is a challenge. You face obstacles from all sides: DOM inconsistencies, faulty language implementations, CSS quirks, weird Ajax bugs, and more. On the server side, once you have a runtime ready, you still face the enormous task of putting together the basic bricks of an application server such as a datastore, a network stack, a module system, and so on.

Fortunately, great people already solved these challenges for you. There's a wealth of options, too, especially on the client side; take a look at Appendix C, on page 115, for details on the main JavaScript frameworks.

Because any competent and *pragmatic* JavaScript developer will rely on one or more good frameworks, this book takes care to illustrate all the major client-side frameworks in what I think of as "basic" tasks. I selected Prototype, jQuery, MooTools, YUI, Dojo, and ExtJS, which should cover most of the "developer mind share" in this business.

---

3.   http://www.opera.com/company/education/curriculum/

For "nonbasic" tasks, I went mostly with my personal favorite, Prototype,[4] except for one task (the lightbox one), where the solution I deem superior ends up being a jQuery plug-in. But really, once you master the basic tasks, you can rewrite or adapt my solutions using your framework of choice. And indeed, to facilitate this, we're putting the entire codebase for this book up in a public GitHub repository.[5] This way, creating a variant favoring another framework (say, jQuery) is as easy as clicking GitHub's Fork button, and finding such derived versions of the codebase becomes a snap.

Also note that all the code for this book, besides being available in a neatly packaged code archive on the book's website,[6] is available live for your testing and tweaking pleasure at http://demos.pocketjavascript.com/.

This Book at a Glance

This book is divided into theme-oriented parts, each with a number of tasks. It concludes with a few appendixes, some of which you may want to read *before* the main body of the book (especially the cheat sheet and the one about debugging JavaScript).

- Part 1 covers a few critical JavaScript code patterns that are too often ignored by JavaScript developers. They're just about the language, so they're framework-agnostic but indispensible for good coding on a daily basis. Be sure to start here!

- Part 2 is mostly about what I refer to as "basic" tasks, focusing on fundamental DOM and CSS manipulations, plus event handling and timers. Because of their "basic" status, I took care to list the relevant code for all major frameworks, so you can pick whatever suits you best. You should also check out Appendix C, on page 115, when reading this part so you get a good picture of the framework landscape and make informed decisions.

- Part 3 is all about the user interface, especially visual effects and neat UI ideas: good-looking tooltips, lightboxes, image preloading, infinite scrolling, and the like.

- Part 4 is complementary to Part 3, because it focuses on forms, a critical part of most web applications. Among other things, a number of tools are there to assist, simplify, and validate input.

- Part 5 is all about the client-server relationship, with topics such as cookies, JSON, and Ajax (same- and cross-domain).

---

4. Full disclosure: I'm a member of Prototype Core.
5. http://github.com/tdd/pragmatic-javascript
6. http://pragprog.com/titles/pg_js

- Part 6, the final part, pushes this idea further by talking with third-party services, in the best mashup spirit. I chose three trendy topics here: playing with Twitter, Flickr, and geo-related APIs.

- Appendix A is my take on a JavaScript cheat sheet; I attempted to condense both the reference of the language and the important tips, leaving out a few language elements I felt were superfluous. I hope you find it useful.

- Appendix B is about debugging JavaScript; you owe it to yourself to know everything inside it, if only to spare you countless hours of hair-tearing, particularly when it comes to Internet Explorer.

- Appendix C tries to provide a useful description of the major frameworks I chose to include in this book. I did my best to provide an accurate depiction of all of them, presenting them in their best light and giving you a few tips about how best to choose a framework, on a case-by-case basis.

- Appendix D acts as a quick reference to the best helpful resources about JavaScript itself and the main frameworks; it sums up the relevant parts of Appendix C, plus a number of extra resources, mostly language-related. I put it at the end of the book so it's easier to locate.

How to Read This Book

In the Pragmatic Guide series, each chapter consists of two facing pages—one with text and one with code. If you're reading this book on paper, this flows naturally. But if you're reading an electronic edition of this book, you may want to set your reader to display two pages at once, in the side-by-side or "two-up" mode, provided your display is large enough. This will give you the best results.

Part I

Bread and Butter: Pure JavaScript

It's time to get started. This part serves as a warm-up with a couple fundamental pieces of know-how about bare-bones JavaScript. The code samples in the following tasks do not rely on any framework or library.

- You'll learn how to access object properties and methods dynamically (once your code decides what their name is) in Task 1, *Dynamically Selecting a Method/Property.*

- In Task 2, *Achieving Code Privacy with the Module Pattern,* you'll find out how to keep internals of your code enclosed in a private scope to avoid "polluting" other code and keep your stuff self-contained.

- Finally, you'll be able to create functions that can be called with a wide variety of arguments, using Task 3, *Using Optional, Variable, and Named Arguments.*

Remember that you can get a full source code archive for this book on its online page.[7] You can also access them directly at the demo site.[8] Finally, don't forget that a simple empty web page (later, with whatever libraries or frameworks you need loaded in), with a JavaScript console open, is all you need to test this stuff interactively.

---

7. http://pragprog.com/titles/pg_js
8. http://demos.pocketjavascript.com

1 Dynamically Selecting a Method/Property

Often you find yourself wanting to call one of two methods (functions associated with an object) depending on the situation. Or instead of functions to call, this could be about reading, or writing, to one of two possible properties (variables associated with an object). The code for this would look something like what follows:

```
if (condition) {
  myObj.method1(someArg);
} else {
  myObj.method2(someArg);
}
```

JavaScript offers a simple syntax for dynamically selecting methods and properties, all relying on the square brackets ([]) operator. You see, JavaScript has two interchangeable syntaxes for member access (that is a common dynamic language trait):

```
obj[expressionResultingInMemberName] == obj.memberName
```

If you've ever plucked a value from an Array cell using its integer index, you've already used the square brackets operator for dynamic member selection! This is because Array objects have properties named after their numerical indices (plus the length property). However, in this case, JavaScript won't let you use the dot operator (.) for direct access. myArray.0 is invalid syntax (too bad, that would have made a good nerd trick).

Here's why using the square brackets operator ([]) is more powerful than dot notation: you can put anything in between the brackets to obtain the name of the member (property or method) that you want to access. Common cases include literals, variables holding the member name, name composition expressions (mostly string concatenations), and quick **if/then** choices in the form of a ternary operator (condition ? valueIfTrue : valueIfFalse). It'll all be turned into a string first and then used to look up the member you want to use.

In JavaScript, functions are objects too and can be referenced like any other value. When an expression results in a function, you can call it by using parentheses, possibly with arguments, just like you would on a function you're calling straight by its name.

Note that if the arguments you want to pass to the method vary depending on which technique you select, using parentheses may quickly become too cluttered for easy reading. In that case, going for a regular **if/else** structure is a wiser move.

► Use the square brackets ([]) operator.

```
object['propertyName']      // => object.propertyName
object['methodName'](arg1)  // => object.methodName(arg1)
```

► Toggle behavior.

```
// Call show() or hide(), depending on shouldBeVisible
element[shouldBeVisible ? 'show' : 'hide']();

// Avoid "heavy" animations on IE to favor immediate reflow
// (assumes we've got a properly set isIE variable)
element[isIE ? 'simpleEffect' : 'complexEffect']();
```

► Compose method names.

```
element[(enable ? 'add' : 'remove') + 'ClassName']('enabled');
```

► Try this example code in any window.

```
var love = { firstName: 'Élodie', lastName: 'Porteneuve' };
var useFirstName = true;
alert(love[useFirstName ? 'firstName' : 'lastName']); // => "Élodie"
```

2 Achieving Code Privacy with the Module Pattern

The more JavaScript there is in your codebase, the more your global scope may get "polluted" with numerous functions and variables that would actually be better kept private to whatever set of code uses it. With this comes the risk of name collision, with one script unintentionally overwriting another's identifiers. This leads to bugs.

We need to be able to create self-contained, opaque batches of JavaScript code, which would expose only selected identifiers, if any, to the outside world. Indeed, this is a major requirement for "programming in the large," being able to bring in frameworks and libraries in any page without risking a clash. This is what the module pattern is for.

The whole idea of the module pattern is to create a private scope for **var**-declared identifiers and functions, a scope that only functions defined inside it can access. To make some of these definitions accessible to the outside world, our enclosing function has two choices. It may return an object with these selected values as properties (see the facing page); we just need to assign that returned object to a variable in the outside scope. Another way is to pass the enclosing function a scope object that it writes properties to (to make these global, you'd simply pass window).

In JavaScript, identifiers first used with the **var** declaring keyword are *local*. (They belong to the function currently defined.) Identifiers first used without **var** are *global*. (They're grafted onto the current default scope, which most of the time means the global window object.)

In a few specific circumstances, the current default scope will not actually be global, so there are ways to execute code in a context where non-**var** identifiers will not leak into the global namespace—but that is a bit outside the scope of this task.

Technically, you do not have to name your "public properties" exactly like your private identifiers. Indeed, you could define public methods on the fly in the returned object literal using anonymous functions. But such practices would result in code that is more obscure (or misleading) to read and—perhaps more importantly—to debug. As a rule of thumb, whenever possible, try to define your functions using *named function expressions*:

```
function myFunctionName(...) { ... }
```

This makes for clearer code and helps a lot with the readability of the stack traces when debugging your JavaScript.

▶ Use **vars** inside anonymous functions.

```
(function() {
  var privateField = 42;

  function innerFunc() {
    notSoPrivate = 43;
    return notSoPrivate;
  }

  alert(privateField); // => 42
  innerFunc();
  alert(notSoPrivate); // => 43
})();
alert(typeof privateField); // => undefined
alert(notSoPrivate); // => 43 (ouch!)
```

▶ Try this example: "private properties."

```
var obj = (function() {
  var privateField = 42;
  var publicField  = 'foobar';

  function processInternals() { alert('Internal stuff: ' + privateField); }

  function run() {
    processInternals();
    alert('Still private stuff: ' + privateField);
    alert('Public stuff: ' + publicField);
  }

  return {
    publicField: publicField,
    run: run
  };
})();

obj.run() // three alerts: Internal, still private, public
obj.publicField // foobar
obj.processInternals() // Undefined
obj.privateField // Undefined
```

3 Using Optional, Variable, and Named Arguments

To master argument-fu, the one thing you must really grok is this: *the parameters you explicitly name do not constrain the arguments you actually pass.* Every function keeps a list of the arguments passed to it in a predefined arguments local variable that behaves like an Array. (It has length and a [] operator.) So, declaring parameters is equivalent to providing local names for the first arguments that may be passed. If arguments are indeed passed in these positions, these identifiers will refer to them. If not, the identifiers will be **undefined**.

Now, pay special attention to the beginning of the optional arguments example on the facing page. We're testing whether a second argument was passed by using an undefined === rant test. Why the triple equal sign? The answer lies in the *equivalence rules* of JavaScript. Check this out:

```
undefined === null // => false
undefined == null  // => true
```

Ah. So, assuming we would consider **null** a valid value for rant, we need to check not only the value but the *type* of rant. That's exactly what === does. It's the *strict equality operator*.

Quite often, though, you'll use a more lax definition of "missing" for your argument. For instance, rant is supposed to be a usable text: empty strings, **null**, **undefined**, 0, and **false** would likely all be considered useless. All of these are *false-equivalent* in JavaScript, so we could get pretty concise here:

```
rant = rant || 'IE6 must die!';
```

This broad range of false-equivalence in JavaScript is the main reason I use the **in** operator in the fourth example on the facing page, to determine whether the options object has a given property already—instead of just testing !options[opt]. This code is fairly generic, and we'd like to be able to use it anywhere, so we're taking a conservative approach and testing actual property presence, regardless of the property's value.

That example also shows the proper use of the **for...in** construct to iterate over an object's *properties*.

Finally, notice the way I defined the defaults for repeat( )'s arguments in a public property of the function itself. This allows our user code to modify the defaults without resorting to a global object that's not syntactically related to our function. To generically grab a reference to our function from *within itself*, we use the special callee property of arguments.

▶ Declare parameters (name arguments).

```
function repeat(rant, times) {
  while (--times >= 0)
    alert(rant);
}
repeat('IE6 must die!', 5); // => 5 alert boxes in a row
```

▶ Grab arguments (however many).

The built-in arguments local variable lets you access them dynamically.
This lets you emulate variable-length argument lists, or *varargs*.

```
function repeat(times) {
  while (--times >= 0) {
    for (var index = 1, len = arguments.length; index < len; ++index) {
      alert(arguments[index]);
    }
  }
}
repeat(2, 'IE6 must die!', 'So should IE7...'); // => 4 alert boxes
```

▶ Take optional arguments with default values.

```
function repeat(times, rant) {
  if (undefined === rant) {
    rant = 'IE6 must die!';
  }
  while (--times >= 0) {
    alert(rant);
  }
}
repeat(3); // => 3 IE6 alert boxes
repeat(3, 'So should IE7...'); // => 3 IE7 alert boxes
```

▶ Use a literal object for pseudo-named arguments.

```
function repeat(options) {
  options = options || {};
  for (var opt in (repeat.defaultOptions || {})) {
    if (!(opt in options)) {
      options[opt] = repeat.defaultOptions[opt];
    }
  }
  for (var index = 0; index < options.times; ++index) {
    alert(options.rant);
  }
}
repeat.defaultOptions = { times: 2, rant: 'IE6 must die!' };

repeat(); // 2 IE6 alert boxes
repeat({ times: 3 }); // 3 IE6 alert boxes
repeat({ times: 2, rant: 'Flash must die!' }); // 2 Flash alert boxes
```

Part II

The DOM, Events, and Timers

So, we started stretching our JavaScript muscles with Part I, focusing on a few key aspects of the language. It is now time to dive into what ties JavaScript and our web pages together: manipulating the DOM.

DOM manipulations mostly fall into a few categories:

- Getting references to the elements we want to manipulate, covered in Task 4, *Obtaining References to DOM Elements*

- Changing their appearance, either instantly or in an animated fashion (most of the time it's about showing, hiding, or moving them), as described in Task 5, *Dynamically Styling Content*

- Altering their contents, which is illustrated in Task 6, *Changing an Element's Contents*

All of this happens either during page initialization, in reaction to specific events, or sometimes after some time has passed. We will therefore discuss the following:

- Page initialization in Task 7, *Running Code When the DOM Is Loaded*. More specifically, we'll discuss how to detect when the DOM is loaded so we can start tweaking it.

- How to listen on events, looking at the basics in Task 8, *Listening for Events (and Stopping)*, then aiming for efficiency with Task 9, *Leveraging Event Delegation*, and finally gaining power with Task 10, *Decoupling Behaviors with Custom Events*.

- How to play with timers (for instance to simulate background processing), in Task 11, *Simulating Background Processing*.

And because they are such critical building blocks of any significant web application, I'm going to show you code for them in all the major frameworks I selected for this book; at this level, they're all functionally equivalent anyway. Compared anatomy was all the rage a couple centuries ago; it still remains a good way to get a wider perspective on things.

4 Obtaining References to DOM Elements

Grabbing elements on a page and "traversing" the DOM (moving around from one element to another) are two cornerstones of any web page scripting. Although the grabbing part is finally being addressed properly in latest crop of browsers—it took more than a decade, though!—DOM walking without libraries remains an incredible mess. That's why we all use one library or another, either consistently or on a per-project basis.

There are only a few points I'd like to touch on here.

First, be warned that all code relying on document.getElementById falls victim to IE's unbelievable quirk. It will look into any and all name= attributes, too. Now, if you work with strict DOCTYPEs (which you should!), this seems to only mean "Beware of field names!" That's because you unconsciously rule out the <head> and its <meta> tag's name= attribute. So, what happens when you unwittingly define an element with an id= of *description* or *keywords* and you try to grab it? You get the <meta> element instead of your intended target! So, just avoid these id= values.

On the facing page, I mention that most techniques for selecting elements let you specify a *context node* or *root node*, which acts as a root element within which to perform the selection. By default, that context is the whole document. If you look at API docs for utilities such as $$( ), query( ), jQuery's all-purpose $( ), and the like, you'll always find an optional argument (usually the second one) that lets you pass your context element. Remember that the narrower the search, the faster the selection!

Finally, the bare-bones DOM API is not well suited to common moving-around use cases, because it works with *nodes*, not *elements*. You get bogged down in whitespace, comments, text nodes, and so on. This is why most libraries provide nifty, element-oriented helpers. Prototype, jQuery, and MooTools provide a rich API, with previous( ) (or prev( )), next( ), siblings( ), ancestors( ), and the like, or get-prefixed versions of these. The YUI 3 API is slightly less rich. Dojo and Ext JS seem to lack this sugar in their cores.

Most libraries support ID- and CSS3-based selections.

▶ Grab an element by its ID.

```
document.getElementById('elementId')  // Plain W3C DOM
$('elementId')                        // Prototype, MooTools
$('#elementId')                       // jQuery
Y.one('#elementId')                   // YUI 3
dojo.byId('elementId')                // Dojo
Ext.getDom('elementId')               // Ext JS 3
```

▶ Grab elements by XPath/CSS selection.

Supported syntaxes vary depending on the library, and the W3C Selectors API is available (but blazingly fast) only in recent-enough browsers: Firefox 3.1+, Safari 3.1+, IE8+ (standards mode), Chrome, and Opera 10+.

Also, note that all libraries provide some way to specify the *context*, the root node within which to explore (by default the entire document). Narrowing the context down whenever possible speeds up your code and reduces memory usage.

```
document.querySelectorAll('selectors')   // Native (see above)
$$('selectors')                          // Prototype, MooTools
someRootElement.select('selectors')      // Prototype
$('selectors')                           // jQuery
Y.all('selectors')                       // YUI 3
dojo.query('selectors')                  // Dojo
Ext.query('selectors')                   // Ext JS 3
```

▶ Move around (DOM traversals).

Here are a couple of quick Prototype-based examples. For context and extra information, check out the facing page.

```
// From element with id=some..., get the nearest <h2> container with class
// "category", then walk along its later sibling elements until one has a
// "summary" class.
$('someDeeplyNestedElement').up('h2.category').next('.summary');

// Set the text-indent CSS property for every immediate container of
// links with a "sifr" class.
$$('a.sifr').invoke('up').invoke('setStyle', 'text-indent: -9999px');
```

5 | Dynamically Styling Content

The ability to get the current value (specified or computed) of a CSS property for an element—and even more importantly to *change* that styling—is of paramount importance when creating a web UI. Unfortunately, browsers and W3C specs leave us pretty much in the dark here. All libraries provide more or less the same API, as you can see on the facing page.

The answer, for dynamic styling, is to use *classes*.

Being able to tweak styles manually is useful for developing your own visual effects, but that's an exercise best left to library authors and JavaScript ninjas. I believe that you, as a front-end developer, should cleanly separate the specific styling from your JavaScript code and rely only on toggling CSS class names for your own stuff and built-in effects provided by your library of choice.

Indeed, all libraries provide a uniform API to add, remove, and check the presence of CSS class names from an element. MooTools, jQuery, YUI, Dojo, and Ext all use addClass( ), hasClass( ), removeClass( ), and toggleClass( ). Prototype just appends a Name suffix to those (that is, hasClassName( )).

But don't forget the shortcuts!

All libraries provide various shortcuts for common use cases, both on the get and the set sides, such as visibility (hide/show/toggle), opacity (as per CSS's spec, even on IE), dimensions, and so on. Check the docs—the method names are often obvious.

▶ Style an element.

```
// Prototype
$(element).setStyle('prop: value; prop2: value2;')
$(element).setStyle({ prop: 'value', prop2: 'value2' })
// jQuery
$(element).css('prop', 'value')
$(element).css({ prop: 'value', prop2: 'value2' })
// MooTools
$(element).setStyle('prop', 'value')
$(element).setStyles({ prop: 'value', prop2: 'value2' })
// YUI 3
Y.one('#id').setStyle('prop', 'value')
Y.one('#id').setStyles({ prop: 'value', prop2: 'value2' })
// Dojo
dojo.style(element, 'prop', 'value')
dojo.style(element, { prop: 'value', prop2: 'value2' })
// Ext JS
Ext.get(element).setStyle('prop', 'value')
Ext.get(element).setStyle({ prop: 'value', prop2: 'value2' })
Ext.get(element).applyStyles(function (e) { return someSpec; })
```

▶ Retrieve a style.

```
// Prototype
$(element).getStyle('prop')
// jQuery
$(element).css('prop')
// MooTools
$(element).getStyle('prop')
// YUI 3
Y.one('#id').getComputedStyle('prop')
Y.one('#id').getStyle('prop')
// Dojo
dojo.style(element, 'prop')
dojo.style(element) // => full computed style set
// Ext JS
Ext.get(element).getStyle('prop')
Ext.get(element).getStyles('prop', 'prop2', 'prop3')
```

Related Tasks

• Task 6, *Changing an Element's Contents*, on the following page

6 | Changing an Element's Contents

You may ask, why not just use innerHTML to change an element's contents?

It is often tempting to just go and assign the desired markup to the innerHTML property of the container element. Indeed, this is orders of magnitude faster than other methods. However, on many browsers, innerHTML chokes on various bits of markup. Libraries switch to other mechanisms (such as manual DOM building or markup preprocessing) when necessary. When dealing with content injection instead of full-on replacement—or when the markup includes inline scripts, as discussed a couple paragraphs later—using libraries also proves easier, more concise, and less error-prone than manually tweaking markup.

Be careful not to confuse *updating* with *replacing*. Most methods do updating by default—for example, the *only* position for dojo.place( ). Updating changes the *inside* of the element, but replacing changes *the element itself*, thereby invalidating its ID and any event listeners attached to it. It is equivalent to setting the outerHTML property, when available.

Fortunately, several libraries provide a wealth of special-case methods supplementing the basic update/insert need, such as element wrapping, selector-based multiple-element operations, cleanup of superfluous empty text nodes, and the like. Be sure to check your preferred library's API documentation for details.

But if you're injecting <*script*> tags, watch out! By default, embedded <*script*> tags in natively injected markup will *not* run, and this is sometimes an issue. Whenever you can, work around this by leveraging event delegation.[9] But this need is common enough that several libraries specifically address it:

- Prototype actually runs inline <*scripts*> by default in update( ), replace( ), and insert( ). (For Ajax updates, you'll need to set the evalScripts option to **true**.)

- jQuery's html( ) method also runs inline scripts by default.

- Ext's update( ) method accepts a second argument that, when **true**, runs inline scripts.

These script runnings sometimes operate within a special evaluation context for security purposes. Check out your preferred library's documentation for details.

---

9. See Task 9, *Leveraging Event Delegation*, on page 24 for details.

► Update the entire contents of an element.

```
// Prototype
$(element).update('<p>new internal HTML</p>')
$(element).replace('<p>This will replace the element itself</p>')
// jQuery
$(element).html('<p>new internal HTML</p>')
$(element).text('The <div> and <span> elements carry no inherent semantics.')
// MooTools
$(element).set('html', '<p>new internal HTML</p>')
$(element).set('text', 'The semantics of << and >> varies across languages.')
// YUI 3
Y.one('#id').setContent('<p>new internal HTML</p>')
// Dojo
dojo.place('<p>new internal HTML</p>', element, 'only')
dojo.place('<p>This will replace the element itself</p>', element, 'replace')
// Ext JS
Ext.get(element).update('<p>new internal HTML</p>')
```

Notice how jQuery and MooTools have special updaters that will escape whatever tags are present in the passed text; this is handy when trying to actually *display code*.

► Inject extra contents into an element.

```
// Prototype. Positions: 'before', 'top', 'bottom', 'after'
$(element).insert('<p>This gets at bottom</p>')
$(element).insert({ pos: markup, pos2: markup2... })
// jQuery (many more methods available)
$(element).before('<p>This gets before the element</p>')
$(element).prepend('<p>This gets at top</p>')
$(element).append('<p>This gets at bottom</p>')
$(element).after('<p>This gets after the element</p>')
// YUI 3
Y.one('#id').prepend('<p>This gets at top</p>')
Y.one('#id').append('<p>This gets at top</p>')
Y.one('#id').insert('<p>This gets where told</p>', nextChildElement)
Y.one('#id').insert('<p>This gets where told</p>', childIndex)
// Dojo. Positions: 'before', 'first', 'last', 'after'
dojo.place('<p>This gets where told</p>', element, pos)
// Ext JS. Positions: 'beforeBegin', 'afterBegin', 'beforeEnd', 'afterEnd'
Ext.get(element).insertHtml(pos, '<p>This gets where told</p>')
```

Related Tasks

• Task 5, *Dynamically Styling Content*, on page 16

7 Running Code When the DOM Is Loaded

Being able to run code as soon as the page's DOM is loaded is a critical part of making your page responsive right from the start.

If you kick in only when the *window's load event* triggers, your code must wait for every last resource to be loaded—style sheets, images, and scripts such as Google Analytics trackers, which can be annoyingly slow. That can amount to a *long* time after the initial page rendering.

All libraries naturally address this topic, in rather similar ways. You end up attaching a function to a custom trigger they provide, through a custom method or a custom event (such as in Prototype, MooTools, and YUI 3).

By the way, here's a related good practice: if parts of your UI rely on JavaScript, you should style your page in such a way that the non-JavaScript alternative is visible by default and the JavaScript-related UI is hidden. Then in the DOM-loaded event, you would just add a JavaScript-related class to your document's body and let your CSS toggle visibilities accordingly. This is *much* better than hiding irrelevant UI through JavaScript, because it avoids the risk of such UI flashing in and out during page load.

Now for a rather technical side note: imagine your initialization code is in an instance method somewhere and that method needs to preserve its binding. It uses **this** internally and needs it to refer to its proper containing instance. Although most libraries let you wing it with a regular method binding (such as with Prototype's bind( )), Dojo and Ext JS address this up front by letting you provide an explicit reference for the method's instance. That way, they can call the method in its proper context directly:

```
// Dojo
dojo.addOnLoad(binding, fx)
// Ext JS
Ext.onReady(fx, binding)
```

You should also check whether your initialization code can actually run at DOM-loading time; in a few situations, this is actually too soon. For instance, you may depend on specific images being loaded so you can set up a UI based on their dimensions, or in a similar vein, you may need to have a CSS style sheet loaded and applied to get proper element dimensions, color, or whatnot. You may then need to wait for window's *load* event. Most of the time, though, DOM-loading is "late enough" and makes a perfect setup spot.

► Trigger at DOM load.

```
// Prototype
document.observe('dom:ready', fx)
// jQuery
$(fx)
// MooTools
window.addEvent('domready', fx)
// YUI 3
Y.on('domready', fx)
// Dojo
dojo.addOnLoad(fx)
// Ext JS
Ext.onReady(fx)
```

Related Tasks

- Task 8, *Listening for Events (and Stopping)*, on the next page

8 Listening for Events (and Stopping)

Events are a *huge* subject, and there's no way this two-page spread will cover even the basics. The main idea is this: what you see on the facing page is a very short reference card. You *should* (I could almost say, you *must*) take the time to carefully read your library's documentation and guides on events. Mastering event-fu will pay off 100 times over.

In particular, note that many libraries have shorthand methods for listening to specific events. So, you could call, say, onclick(handlerFx) instead of connect('click', handlerFx). Another useful trick is that most libraries let you pass fewer arguments when you stop observing, decommissioning all events that match that broader spec (all click handlers or all of the element's handlers, for example).

Noteworthy specifics: Dojo uses a single mechanism to connect any sort of event (regular DOM event, custom events, so-called global events, publish-subscribe stuff, and bare-bones *method calls*) to the triggering of any sort of function (bona fide event handlers, plain functions, and methods). This is pretty nifty. And Ext allows a fourth argument to on( ), which allows a wealth of options.

Should you want to observe events at the document level (leveraging event bubbling), all libraries provide an easy way to do so. For instance, Prototype lets you call document.observe, and there are wrappers like dojo.doc and Ext.getDoc( ). However, you should not rely too much on arguments and options related to *event capture* (top-down event propagation/censorship), because they are often not properly supported on IE before IE8.

All libraries also take care to provide your handlers with a beefed-up Event object, equipped with W3C-mandated properties and methods and often a few more, to boot.

By default, handler functions, being passed as function references, lose their potential binding and execute in the global context.[10] Several libraries address this on the spot, letting you pass an optional scope object argument.

Finally, most libraries support custom events and bake a few ones in, mainstream or otherwise. I know I couldn't live without DOM readiness, *mouseenter*, and *mouseleave*, to name but a few.

---

10. For the whole story on JavaScript binding—its gotchas and tricks—check out my ALA article at http://www.alistapart.com/articles/getoutbindingsituations/.

► Listen to an event on one element.

```
// Prototype
$(element).observe('event', handlerFx)
// jQuery
$(elementOrSelector).bind('event', handlerFx)
// MooTools
$(element).addEvent('event', handlerFx)
// YUI 3
Y.on('event', handlerFx, elementOrSelector)
// Dojo (context-free handlerFx or context-requiring method)
dojo.connect(element, 'event', handlerFx)
// Ext
Ext.get(element).on('event', handlerFx)
```

► Listen to an event on multiple elements.

```
// Prototype
elements.invoke('observe', 'event', handlerFx)
// jQuery
$(elements).bind('event', handlerFx)
// YUI 3
Y.on('event', handlerFx, elementOrSelector)
// Dojo
dojo.query(selector).connect('event', handlerFx)
// Ext, for on-DOM-readiness bindings:
Ext.addBehaviors({ 'selector@event': handlerFx... })
```

► Stop listening.

```
// Prototype
$(element).stopObserving('event', handlerFx)
// jQuery
$(elementOrSelector).unbind('event', handlerFx)
// MooTools
$(element).removeEvent('event', handlerFx)
// YUI 3
Y.detach('event', handlerFx, elementOrSelector)
// Dojo
dojo.disconnect(handleReturnedByConnect)
// Ext (watch out: "un", not "on"...)
Ext.get(element).un('event', handlerFx)
```

Related Tasks

- Task 7, *Running Code When the DOM Is Loaded*, on page 20
- Task 9, *Leveraging Event Delegation*, on the next page
- Task 10, *Decoupling Behaviors with Custom Events*, on page 26

9 | Leveraging Event Delegation

Learn this by heart, and make it yours: *event delegation is the better way.*

You see, most events *bubble*, such as mouse or keyboard events. When they happen somewhere in the DOM, they trigger on every element along the ancestor line, up to the document element, from the inside out (that is, unless one of these elements has a listener that stops the bubbling).

Suppose we have a large number of elements that should share a behavior. If the triggering event for that behavior bubbles, we're much better off listening for it higher up in the DOM, at the level of the elements' nearest common ancestor or perhaps directly at the document level. This saves some significant memory and CPU time.

Listening higher up in the DOM is also great for behaviors on Ajax-loaded contents. Because you listen "outside" the loaded content, freshly added elements leverage your behavior automatically, without requiring post-load listener attachment.

However, sometimes we have to resort to hacks or abandon delegation entirely, because our triggering events do not bubble. Unbelievably, submit, change, focus, and blur do not bubble—this is infuriating when dealing with shared form/field behavior. Although workaround code exists to simulate bubbling for at least part of these, their inability to bubble is a hassle.

I should mention that only since jQuery 1.4 did live( ) become flexible enough for event delegation per se, without performance issues. With that version, it also gained the ability to work on many nonbubbling events. On the other hand, Dojo's behavior( ) seems like it would use event delegation, but it doesn't. It's just nice syntactic sugar.

Note the findElement( ) call in the code sample, on line 2. Currently, our links just contain a simple text, so clicking *within* the link means clicking the link itself. But imagine you jazz things up and add an icon (such as a plus/minus icon). Then clicks could, technically, happen on the *icon* but still within the link. So with Prototype, when you attach a delegation-based event listener, be sure to always use the event's findElement( ) method instead of its less witty element( ) counterpart.

► Toggle item contents.

`dom/delegation.html`

```html
<ul id="items">
  <!-- We will insert togglers in each LI using JS -->
  <li><div><p>Data 1</p><p>Data 2</p></div></li>
  <li><div><p>Data 1</p><p>Data 2</p></div></li>
  <li><div><p>Data 1</p><p>Data 2</p></div></li>
  <!-- Potentially lots more elements here... -->
</ul>
```

Here's a Prototype-based script for it:

`dom/delegation.js`

```
Line 1   $('items').observe('click', function(e) {
    -      var trigger = e.findElement('a.toggler');
    -      if (!trigger) return;
    -      e.stop();
    5      var content = trigger.up('p').next('div');
    -      if (!content) return;
    -      content.toggle();
    -      trigger.update(content.visible() ? 'Close' : 'Open');
    -      trigger.blur();
   10    });
    -
    -    $('items').select('li').each(function(item) {
    -      item.insert({ top: '<p><a class="toggler" href="#">Open</a></p>' });
    -      item.down('div').hide();
   15    });
```

► Use a delegation-specific API in libraries.

```
// Prototype 1.7
$('items').on('click', 'a.toggler', handlerFx);
// jQuery 1.4
$('a.toggler', '#items').live('click', handlerFx);
// YUI 3
Y.delegate('click', handlerFx, '#items', 'a.toggler');
// Ext
Ext.get('items').on('click', handlerFx, this, { delegate: 'a.toggler' });
```

Related Tasks

- Task 8, *Listening for Events (and Stopping)*, on page 22

10 Decoupling Behaviors with Custom Events

When your codebase grows large enough or when you want to reuse part of it in a totally different context, you may encounter situations where you say, "I wish this code could be triggered any which way, instead of making assumptions about my DOM."

Most of the time, this relates to how widgets can interact with each other. For instance, some background chat polling engine notifies the chat widget new messages are coming in, or a photo viewer and its zoom-preloading facility both get notified when a photo carousel has one of its pictures clicked.

This is what custom events are for. There are several aspects about custom event behavior that will vary depending on which framework you're using:

- *DOM-like behavior*: You listen for and trigger custom events on DOM nodes (including document). They bubble, can get stopped, and so on. This is what Prototype, jQuery, and MooTools do. When events do not propagate, they must be fired on the object listening for them.

- *Namespacing*: Some frameworks will require you to namespace your events, usually with a colon-based prefix, to distinguish them from native events. Prototype mandates this; other frameworks will let you name custom events any way you like.

- *Custom payload*: Frameworks let you pass extra data to the event handler when you trigger the custom event. Prototype accepts a single extra argument (which can obviously be a richly structured object) that will be provided as the event's memo property. jQuery will pass along any extra arguments to the handler, after its initial event object argument. All other frameworks will pass these arguments to the handler without any prefixing. Dojo systematically requires such arguments as a single array, even if there is only one value.

- *Common event API*: Only Dojo seems to require that you use the specific publish/subscribe API for custom events, reserving its usual events API for native DOM events. This also means there is no DOM-like behavior (for instance, bubbling).

- *Declaration*: MooTools lets you define custom events as special variations of predefined events (say, a click requiring the `Alt` key be pressed), yet its facility for declaring such events is mandatory for custom events, even if you should just declare their name. Any undeclared custom event will not be fired.

▶ Listen for a custom event.

```
// Prototype -- payload in event.memo
$(element).observe('ns:event', handlerFx)
document.observe('ns:event', handlerFx)
// jQuery -- payload as handler extra arguments
$(elementOrSelector).bind('event', handlerFx)
// MooTools -- payload as handler arguments
Element.Events.event = {};
$(element).addEvent('event', handlerFx)
// YUI 3 -- payload as handler arguments
Y.on('event', handlerFx)
// Dojo -- payload as handler arguments
dojo.subscribe('event', context, handlerFx)
```

▶ Fire a custom event.

```
// Prototype
$(element).fire('custom:event');
document.fire('custom:event');
whichever.fire('custom:event', { foo: 'bar', baz: 42 });
// jQuery
$(elements).trigger('event')
$(elements).trigger('event', { foo: 'bar', baz: 42 });
$(elements).trigger('event', ['bar', 42]);
// MooTools
$(element).fireEvent('event')
$(element).fireEvent('event', arg)
document.fireEvent('event', [arg1, arg2, arg3])
// YUI 3
Y.fire('event')
Y.fire('event', arg1, arg2, arg3)
// Dojo
dojo.publish('event')
dojo.publish('event', [arg])
```

Related Tasks

- Task 8, *Listening for Events (and Stopping)*, on page 22

11 Simulating Background Processing

Say you need to carry out lengthy processing in your web page; perhaps you intend to provide a computationally intensive, graphical representation of a large dataset from a table. You want to keep the browser responsive while crunching numbers and drawing stuff. This calls for background processing.

This is because of how JavaScript engines execute your code:

- JavaScript is essentially *single-threaded*.

- Your JavaScript-running thread is, for all intents and purposes, shared with the rest of your page's behavior. The immediate consequence is that when your JavaScript code runs, *no rendering happens*. No new content, no reflow, no redrawing of a page partially obscured by another window...nothing.

So, if you run some intensive processing, your page will freeze until that processing completes. That usually means your *entire browser* will freeze. That's why several browsers nowadays have "abort lengthy script" mechanisms in place. Others, such as Chrome, mitigate this issue by running every page in its own process.

Unless you go with Web Workers (which is certainly not a cross-browser option for now), you need to resort to pseudo-parallel tricks, and the main trick relies on a pair of methods—setTimeout( ) and clearTimeout( )—provided by the global window object.

The idea is to partition a big job into any number of smaller steps, keeping track of our progress, knowing when to stop, and scheduling chunks at regular intervals. When a chunk is done, that chunk schedules the next one for a short time later; in the meantime, the browser regains control, thereby being able to handle page activity and any other scripting that needs to run.

Although calling clearTimeout( ) and cleaning up the timer handle you stored from your setTimeout( ) call are not strictly required, both actions are good practice, reduce memory leaks, and have virtually no performance cost.

This technique is great for going through a large processing job, but it's terrible for behaviors demanding a smooth progression—such as visual effects—since timer precision varies wildly (25–500 ms). In such situations, you should use a single fixed-interval timer and rely on time differences for accurate measurement.[11]

---

11. For a real example of this, check out the main loop of Thomas Fuch's awesome Émile, a 50-line visual effects library at http://github.com/madrobby/emile.

▶ Schedule and cancel execution of code.

These are the two core methods at the heart of simulating background
processing with timers:

```
var handle = window.setTimeout(callback, intervalInMs);
window.clearTimeout(handle);
```

▶ Let your user toggle background processing.

This book's source archive includes a visual demo. The crux of the code
goes like this:

dom/background.js

```
var CHUNK_INTERVAL = 25; // ms.
var running = false, progress = 0, processTimer;

function runChunk() {
  window.clearTimeout(processTimer);
  processTimer = null;
  if (!running) return;
  // Some work chunk.  Let's simulate it:
  for (var i = 0; i < 10000; i += (Math.random() * 5).round())
    ;
  ++progress;
  updateUI(); // See source archive -- just updates a progressbar
  if (progress < 100) {
    processTimer = window.setTimeout(runChunk, CHUNK_INTERVAL);
  } else {
    progress = 0, running = false;
  }
}

function toggleProcessing() {
  running = !running;
  if (running) {
    processTimer = window.setTimeout(runChunk, CHUNK_INTERVAL);
  }
}
```

Part III

UI Tricks

Manipulating the DOM is akin to our basic tools. Ultimately, everything else boils down to DOM tweaking. But most of our actual needs are higher level than that, including creating useful user interface (UI) effects, behaviors, and widgets; handling forms in a useful manner; and much more still. In this part, we will start with generally useful UI behaviors.

- Task 12, *Pulling Off Classy Tooltips*, will explore how to provide nice-looking, contextual information "bubbles" in our pages.

- Sometimes pop-up windows *are* OK; and when they are, lack of JavaScript should not prevent access to the target contents. See how to get the best of both worlds in Task 13, *Making Unobtrusive Pop-Ups*.

- Preloading images cannot always be done with CSS spriting (for instance, with user-provided images); for such situations, Task 14, *Preloading Images*, shows you how to resort to JavaScript.

- Proper use of lightboxes (pseudo-dialogs standing out by dimming the remainder of the page) creates a neat experience; Task 15, *Creating a Lightbox Effect*, shows a top-notch solution.

- Browsing large datasets is sometimes better done through smart scrolling, as illustrated in Task 16, *Implementing an "Infinite Scroll"*.

- There are times when you need to load new content *above* the position in the page that triggers such loading; to avoid destabilizing visual behavior, check out Task 17, *Maintaining Viewport When Loading Content*.

From then on in this book, we will rely on frameworks and libraries to ease our work; almost all of the time, I will go with Prototype (the lightbox task will use a jQuery plug-in, though, because it seemed like the best tool for that particular job).

Still, Prototype does not necessarily appeal to every front-end developer out there, so check out the GitHub repository for this book's codebase.[12] I intend for people to create forks of it adapted for whatever JavaScript framework they like best. This way, you can get the code for these tasks in whatever framework you prefer. And if it's not there yet, why not go ahead and author it yourself?

---

12. http://github.com/tdd/pragmatic-javascript

12 Pulling Off Classy Tooltips

Native tooltips (obtained through title=) are unreliable at best. Text wrapping vs. stretching vs. truncation, line breaks, and appearance delays are all browser- or user-dependent. Plus, their content is plain text—no styling and certainly no rich markup.

To reclaim control, we need to implement our own tooltips, positioning elements that get shown or hidden when the mouse enters or exits specific areas of the page (or when the user tabs through, for better accessibility).

Since this book is about JavaScript, I won't delve into the CSS parts. Also, I'll limit the design approach to simple stuff: not overlaying the trigger element, not moving alongside the mouse cursor, not providing in-tooltip mouse-based UI, and so on.

So, for our purposes, the crux of the implementation is this: use CSS to hide the tooltip by default, and add a :hover selector on the container element (which doesn't have to be a link) to restore its visibility.

However, that implementation won't work with IE6, which only obeys :hover on <a> elements. You must use a script to react to mouseover and mouseout manually. Here, because of the way Prototype implements show() and hide(), we can't prehide tooltips through CSS rules—this explains the small IE6 hack I show in the sample CSS on the facing page.

For advanced needs, odds are you'll find your fit among the host of tooltip libraries out there, either directly in frameworks or based on them. Personally, my favorite Prototype-based library is the kick-ass Prototip2.[13]

---

13. http://www.nickstakenburg.com/projects/prototip2/

▶ Tag the tooltip.

`ui/tooltips/index.html`

```html
<li tabindex="1">
  <span class="name">Capacity: 1.5 TB</span>
  <div class="tooltip" >
    <p><strong>1.5 Terabyte = 1,536 Gigabytes</strong></p>
    <p>Enough for 50,000 songs, 1,000 DivX movies, 100,000
      high-definition photos, hundreds of iDVD projects and
      plenty of backup space left.</p>
  </div>
</li>
```

▶ Style the tooltip.

`ui/tooltips/tooltips.css`

```css
#files li { position: relative; }
#files li .tooltip {
  position: absolute; top: 8px; left: 120px; width: 24em;
  z-index: 1; display: none;
  /* IE6 doesn't know li:hover, so we need to toggle via JS,
     therefore avoiding in-rule display: none */
  _display: block;
  border: 1px solid gray;
  background: #fffdc3 url(bg_tooltip.png) top left repeat-x;
}
#files li:hover .tooltip,
#files li:focus .tooltip { display: block; }
```

▶ Script for IE6 (which won't :hover on nonlinks).

`ui/tooltips/tooltips.js`

```javascript
function toggle(reveal, e) {
  var trigger = e.findElement('li'),
    tooltip = trigger && trigger.down('.tooltip');
  if (!tooltip) return;
  tooltip[reveal ? 'show' : 'hide']();
}

document.observe('dom:loaded', function() {
  var isIE6 = Prototype.Browser.IE &&
    undefined === document.body.style.maxHeight;
  if (!isIE6) return;
  var files = $('files'), tooltips = files && files.select('.tooltip');
  if (!files || 0 == tooltips.length) return;
  tooltips.invoke('hide');
  files.observe('mouseover', toggle.curry(true)).
    observe('mouseout', toggle.curry(false));
});
```

13 Making Unobtrusive Pop-Ups

Whether you're using "actual" pop-ups (distinct windows) or pseudo pop-ups (elements on the current page, styled to look window-like), the problem remains: how do you provide access to this content for users who can't—or don't want to—open a window? Think disabled window opening, screen readers, search engines, and so on.

There's only one way: have the link *actually link to* the pop-up's contents, and apply progressive enhancement from there.

If your content is intended as an HTML fragment displayed in a pseudo pop-up (perhaps loaded through Ajax, too), you'll need to make sure you can serve it distinctly, with or without a containing document markup. That way, users accessing it through a regular link, as a stand-alone document, get something nice.

The gist of the practice here is this: link to the target content natively (href= and, perhaps, target="_blank"), and then use JavaScript to hook into these links and jazz 'em up. Baking your own window-opening code is fairly easy—it's all about the built-in window.open( ) method.

If you're adding a pseudo pop-up or lightbox, do use a good existing library and spare yourself the living hell of cross-browser issues and positioning algorithms. Here are a few pointers:

- Scripty2's UI part[14]

- jQuery UI[15]

- Dijit (based on Dojo)[16]

- YUI's Overlay module[17]

- Ext.Window[18]

Also keep in mind that small pop-up content may qualify for a click-triggered rich tooltip instead of a full-on pop-up zone. In such a situation, check out tooltip libraries and modules.

---

14. http://github.com/madrobby/scripty2
15. http://jqueryui.com/
16. http://dojotoolkit.org/projects/dijit
17. http://developer.yahoo.com/yui/3/overlay/
18. http://www.extjs.com/deploy/dev/docs/?class=Ext.Window

▶ Tag for progressive enhancement.

`ui/popups/index.html`

```html
<p>
  The great thing about <a class="popup" target="_blank"
  href="http://pragprog.com/titles/pg_js">Pocket Guide to JavaScript</a>
  is that it focuses on a bunch of specific, useful tasks.</p>
```

▶ Script a plain window.open( ).

`ui/popups/popups.js`

```javascript
var POPUP_FEATURES = 'status=yes,resizable=yes,scrollbars=yes,' +
  'width=800,height=500,left=100,top=100';

function hookPopupLink(e) {
  var trigger = e.findElement('a.popup');
  if (!trigger) return;
  e.stop(); trigger.blur();
  var wndName = trigger.readAttribute('target') ||
    ('wnd' + trigger.identify());
  window.open(trigger.href, wndName, POPUP_FEATURES).focus();
}

document.observe('click', hookPopupLink);
```

Related Tasks

- Task 12, *Pulling Off Classy Tooltips*, on page 34
- Task 15, *Creating a Lightbox Effect*, on page 40

14 Preloading Images

When your page offers user interaction that changes what images are displayed (perhaps providing a zoom, a close-up, a front/back view, or whatever), you do not want the user to see a momentary blank screen because the image you suddenly need takes an instant to load. You may want to preload such images.

In essence, there are only three ways to preload images:

- *With JavaScript, using dynamically created* Image *objects with appropriate* src *properties*: Doing so lets you detect when preloaded images are *indeed* loaded.

- *With CSS, hiding preloaded images*: This boils down to using hidden <img> tags for the images to preload. You hide either the <img> tags themselves or a common container (which I prefer).

- *With CSS sprites*: When you want to preload stuff like rollovers or a bunch of related images (backgrounds, borders, and corners, for instance), this should definitely be your preferred approach.[19]

The CSS approach is fairly straightforward, but it does not provide you with as much potential control as the JavaScript approach. The markup and script on the facing page make the assumption that image tags with a rel="preloadZoom" attribute have a close-up version with the same URI—with a *_closeup* name suffix—preloaded for rollover close-ups.

This is typically the kind of situation where the JavaScript option is preferable to the CSS ones. Since the rollover depends on JavaScript, we should preload in JavaScript too. (If no JavaScript is available, we won't preload stuff that can't be shown later.) Moreover, preloading in JavaScript avoids markup/styling bloat.

With JavaScript, we can avoid the risk of a temporarily blank/incomplete render by toggling to an image only when we're sure it's preloaded. The nonsprite CSS approach runs a (admittedly low) risk of toggling to an image that is not loaded yet.

For more hardcore techniques on fast image loading, take a look at Steve Souder's May 2009 presentation: *14 rules for faster-loading images.*[20]

---

19. Check out the seminal http://www.alistapart.com/articles/sprites and the more recent http://css-tricks.com/css-sprites/. Steve Souders also maintains the SpriteMe tool: http://spriteme.org/.
20. http://stevesouders.com/docs/wordcamp-20090530.ppt

► Tag for preload.

`ui/preloading/index.html`

```html
<ul id="products">
  <li><h2><a href="http://pragprog.com/titles/cppsu">
    <img rel="preloadZoom" src="cppsu.jpg" alt="" />
    <span>Prototype and script.aculo.us</span>
  </a></h2></li>
  <li><h2><a href="http://pragprog.com/titles/vsscala">
    <img rel="preloadZoom" src="vsscala.jpg" alt="" />
    <span>Programming Scala</span>
  </a></h2></li>
</ul>
```

► Script the preload.

`ui/preloading/preloading.js`

```javascript
function preloadImages() {
  $$('img[rel="preloadZoom"]').each(function(img) {
    var pimg = new Image();
    pimg.src = img.src.replace(/(\.\w+$)/, '_closeup$1');
  });
}

document.observe('dom:loaded', preloadImages);
```

► Roll over to (ideally preloaded) images.

`ui/preloading/preloading.js`

```javascript
function togglePreloaded(e) {
  var trigger = e.findElement('img[rel="preloadZoom"]');
  if (!trigger) return;
  if (e.type == 'mouseover') {
    trigger.src = trigger.src.replace(/(\.\w+$)/, '_closeup$1');
  } else {
    trigger.src = trigger.src.replace('_closeup', '');
  }
}

document.observe('mouseover', togglePreloaded).
  observe('mouseout', togglePreloaded);
```

15 Creating a Lightbox Effect

Lightboxing is the act of bringing up some content while shadowing the rest of the page behind a mouse-inhibiting overlay. Most of the time, the lightbox UI is centered on the page. Lightboxes usually feature images and are launched from linked text or a linked thumbnail image on the page.

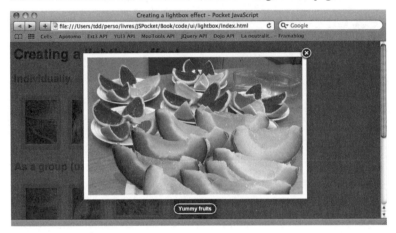

In the example for this book, we're using the FancyBox jQuery plug-in by Janis Skarnelis to make thumbnail images lightbox to larger versions. It's unobtrusive, is fairly lightweight, is drop-in easy, and looks gorgeous out of the box. Still, check out the bottom of the book's demo page for alternatives, if you'd like.

FancyBox is not limited to image contents—it can bring up anything, including *<iframe>* stuff. It defaults to just-in-time Ajax loading when the link's target URI neither "looks like an image file" nor uses iframes. So, fat images can load on-demand through an extensionless URL, for example.

Like most UI-related libraries, FancyBox needs to load at least one script and one CSS file. It assumes its images are in the style sheet's folder, avoiding tedious CSS tweaking. FancyBox makes no image URL requirements.

To make links lightbox, we just grab them and call their fancybox( ) method, as demonstrated on the facing page. It works without any options, but it provides a number of possible tweaks. I really like to see my thumbnails zoom in to their larger versions, so I set it up that way.

► Load FancyBox.

`ui/lightbox/index.html`

```
<link rel="stylesheet" type="text/css"
  href="vendor/fancybox/jquery.fancybox-1.2.6.css" />
<script type="text/javascript" src="vendor/jquery-1.3.2.min.js"></script>
<script type="text/javascript"
  src="vendor/fancybox/jquery.fancybox-1.2.6.pack.js"></script>
```

► Link to individual images.

`ui/lightbox/index.html`

```
<a href="beach_normal.jpg" title="A gorgeous beach">
  <img src="beach.jpg" alt="Beach" />
</a>
```

► Link to images as a browsable group.

`ui/lightbox/index.html`

```
<li>
  <a href="beach_normal.jpg" rel="demo" title="A gorgeous beach">
    <img src="beach.jpg" alt="Beach" />
  </a>
</li>
<li>
  <a href="feline_normal.jpg" rel="demo" title="A cute cub">
    <img src="feline.jpg" alt="Feline" />
  </a>
</li>
```

► Initialize FancyBox (with some customization thrown in).

`ui/lightbox/lightbox.js`

```
$(function() {
  $('#thumbnails a').fancybox({
    zoomSpeedIn: 300, zoomOpacity: true, overlayColor: '#000',
    overlayOpacity: 0.6
  });
});
```

Related Tasks

- Task 12, *Pulling Off Classy Tooltips*, on page 34
- Task 13, *Making Unobtrusive Pop-Ups*, on page 36

16 Implementing an "Infinite Scroll"

Gmail introduced us to infinite scroll, spelling doom for pagination in a number of scenarios. Many people (certainly not all, though) find it more efficient to scroll through a boatload of items and use visual pattern matching rather than pointing to and clicking pagination link after pagination link.

Pagination mostly arose for technical reasons alone:

- Older browsers render slowly, forcing us to keep our pages "light enough."

- Bandwidth may be limited anywhere between client and server, encouraging us to stay lean.

- Server-side processing time grows as the data grows. Rendering the entire dataset *all at once* is not only unnecessary from a consumption standpoint but is infeasible for our servers (or at the very least impractical and unwieldy), especially if they want to keep handling enough concurrent requests.

Still, pagination was just one way—the non-JavaScript way. But as soon as JavaScript is enabled, you can hide any pagination links and replace them with infinite scroll when that makes sense. I leave that decision to your usability experts—and to your good sense.

As you can see on the facing code, infinite scroll is nothing too fancy. The only tricky part is jumping through a couple of hoops to get our metrics right, across browsers, as evidenced in the lowEnough( ) method code.

We check, essentially, that the bottom of the document is not too far below the bottom of our viewport. Then it's just a matter of looking at the current state of vertical scrolling often enough—ten times per second is certainly snappy!—and loading more content through Ajax.

From an accessibility (and failover) perspective, you may want to *also* offer pagination and perhaps hide Next links at setup time and then restore these links if your Ajax fetching fails so users get an alternative.

A note for those of you without a working PHP setup handy: you'll just end up loading more stuff instantaneously; the PHP code simulates load time by waiting half a second before returning static content.

▶ Check whether we scrolled low enough.

`ui/infinite/infinite.js`

```javascript
function lowEnough() {
  var pageHeight = Math.max(document.body.scrollHeight,
    document.body.offsetHeight);
  var viewportHeight = window.innerHeight ||
    document.documentElement.clientHeight ||
    document.body.clientHeight || 0;
  var scrollHeight = window.pageYOffset ||
    document.documentElement.scrollTop ||
    document.body.scrollTop || 0;
  // Trigger for scrolls within 20 pixels from page bottom
  return pageHeight - viewportHeight - scrollHeight < 20;
}
```

▶ Keep an eye on scroll level and fetch more.

`ui/infinite/infinite.js`

```javascript
function checkScroll() {
  if (!lowEnough()) return pollScroll();
  $('spinner').show();
  new Ajax.Updater('posts', 'more.php', {
    method: 'get', insertion: 'bottom',
    onComplete: function() { $('spinner').hide(); },
    onSuccess: pollScroll
  });
}

function pollScroll() { setTimeout(checkScroll, 100); }

pollScroll();
```

17 Maintaining Viewport When Loading Content

At times, you may want to maintain the contents of the user's viewport—all that's visible inside the browser window—even as the user clicks to load more content above it. For example, a user clicks to view previous comments, but you don't want to push the user's scroll position down as the comments load from above.

In cases like this, you'll find yourself facing a small obstacle. Intuitively, users expect that their position on the page will not move. But by loading content above, you'll push the rest of the document, including the clicked zone, farther down the viewport and quite possibly *outside* of it.

The solution is to *preserve the scrolling position relative to the viewport*. To do that, we need to grab the viewport's "scrolling offset"—the viewport position prior to loading content above some of what it displays—and restore that offset once the content has been injected. Offsets are typically a messy business, full of cross-browser hairiness, but thanks to libraries such as Prototype and their position-related features, this can actually be solved rather concisely.

The facing code is adapted from Gist by Sam Stephenson. Before loading extra content, we grab the trigger link's in-document position (its cumulativeOffset( )) and subtract from it the viewport's current scrolling, which tells us how far down this trigger appears *in the viewport*. Then, after the new content is injected, we determine what the viewport's new offset should be, by using the converse subtraction.

Readers familiar with Prototype may wonder why I went with Ajax.Request here, instead of the more specific Ajax.Updater. I did so because this lets me grab the original scrolling position as late as possible, specifically *after the Ajax request completes*, avoiding a weird "scroll reset" effect if the user scrolls during the Ajax request.

This makes for a fairly nice user experience, with very little code.

▶ Preserve the viewport position.

`ui/viewport/index.html`

```html
<h2>Comments</h2>

<div id="extraComments">
  <a id="loadKnownComments" href="?with_known_comments">See previous
    comments you already know about</a>
</div>

<h3>Comment 5</h3>
<p>Lorem ipsum dolor sit amet, consectetur adipisicing elit, sed do
  eiusmod tempor incididunt ut labore et dolore magna aliqua. Ut enim
  ad minim veniam, quis nostrud exercitation ullamco laboris nisi ut
  aliquip ex ea commodo consequat.</p>
```

▶ Grab the scroll before Ajax, and adjust after it.

`ui/viewport/viewport.js`

```javascript
function loadKnownComments(e) {
  e.stop();
  var zone = $('extraComments'), ref = zone.next('h3');
  var upd = new Ajax.Request('known_comments.html', {
    method: 'get',
    onSuccess: function(res) {
      var orig = ref.cumulativeOffset().top -
        document.viewport.getScrollOffsets().top;
      zone.insert({ before: res.responseText });
      window.scrollTo(0, ref.cumulativeOffset().top - orig);
    }
  });
}
```

Part IV

Form-fu

Forms are a key part of web applications now. We are always gathering information from our users to fill in profiles, set up tasks and services, send messages, and whatnot. Yet most of the forms you encounter online are in a sorry state of usability and ergonomics. This part attempts to provide a number of recipes to make user experience (increasingly known as UX) better when dealing with forms.

The key idea behind useful forms is this: don't waste your users' time.

- Save them from double submits, using Task 18, *Temporarily Disabling a Submit Button*.
- Let them know how much text they can still type in, thanks to Task 19, *Providing Input Length Feedback*.
- Allow them to toggle choices on and off en masse, as shown in Task 20, *(Un)checking a Whole Set of Checkboxes at Once*.
- Validate immediately as much of their input as possible, with Task 21, *Validating Forms: The Basics*; Task 22, *Validating Forms: Going Further*; and Task 23, *Validating Forms: The Whole Nine Yards*. Do you know anybody who likes to discover belatedly that their username is already taken or that their password does not comply with security requirements?
- Provide extra help for filling in particular fields, as illustrated in Task 24, *Providing On-the-Fly Help Tooltips on Forms*.
- Suggest alternative inputs or completions; you'll see how in Task 25, *Autocompleting Input As It's Typed*.
- Let them upload multiple files in one pass, a trick that's demonstrated in Task 26, *Using Dynamic Multiple File Uploads*.

Those are just a few examples of what you can do to make your forms more pleasant to use. We will explore how to achieve such things in the following tasks.

Still, never forget that you *cannot* take JavaScript for granted. All your forms should still work with no JavaScript whatsoever; perhaps they will be less nifty to use, but they must work. The server side must validate everything no matter what, no links should lead nowhere when they are not intercepted by scripts, and so on. When putting up forms, *progressive enhancement* is paramount. Make sure they work without scripting or CSS, and then you can add layers of extra comfort through whatever technologies are available—and enabled.

18 Temporarily Disabling a Submit Button

Sometimes our forms take a while to be processed on the server side. Perhaps we're uploading a large file using a good ol' <input type="file"... /> field, or the server is just busy for some reason. At any rate, we do not want our user to resubmit the form while we're processing it already. Double-submits are just irritating, you know?

To avoid this, we can react to our form being submitted by *disabling* any UI means of submitting it, which boils down to *<input>* or *<button>* tags with type="submit" or type="image" attributes. Because a few browsers (such as our beloved MSIE) do not handle CSS attribute selectors well, we should "tag" those elements with a specific class, say *submit*, and use it to select elements we intend to disable.

On the facing page, the first script shows the minimum Prototype-based code for that. It's fairly straightforward.

You will likely want to go the extra mile and add some further UI decoration to your form as it is submitting; not all browsers render disabled fields in a clear visual style, and perhaps you also want to stress the fact that *something is going on*. (You're not just disabling that thing to be obnoxious, are you?)

The second script illustrates adding a custom class to our disabled *<input>* tags. Because the UI update that results from applying CSS is not as "built-in" as a disabling call, we also want to make sure our browser can "take a breath" before we have it submit the form (at which time it's likely to ignore any further visual update and just plow ahead with the submission). To solve this common problem, we delay( ) the submit( ) call by just a tenth of a second.

Also notice the that = this closure trick in our JavaScript code here. As you may know, calling a function (in this case, the one we end up delay( )ing) can lose our current *binding*—the value **this** refers to. Instead of forcing such a binding, which requires an extra layer of function wrapping and is therefore pretty costly, we rely on *closures* to let the code inside our ad hoc anonymous function retain a reference to our original **this** (the form being submitted) in order to call submit( ) on it in due time.[21]

---

21. Queasy about JS function bindings? Check out my ALA article at http://www.alistapart.com/articles/getoutbindingsituations/ for details. Not too sure about closures and how they're useful? My pal Juriy "Kangax" Zaytsev wrote a great article about it at http://msdn.microsoft.com/en-us/scriptjunkie/ff696765.aspx.

▶ Disable on the submit event.

`form/submit/submit.js`

```javascript
function preventMultipleSubmits() {
  this.select('.submit').invoke('disable');
}

document.observe('dom:loaded', function() {
  $('commentForm').observe('submit', preventMultipleSubmits);
});
```

`form/submit/index.html`

```html
<form id="commentForm" action="post_comment.php">
  <p>
    <label for="edtText">Your text</label>
    <textarea id="edtText" name="text" cols="40" rows="5"></textarea>
  </p>
  <p><input type="submit" class="submit" value="Send" /></p>
</form>
```

▶ Use classes for extra decoration (a bit of flourish).

`form/submit/submit.js`

```javascript
function preventMultipleSubmits(e) {
  if (!this.hasClassName('submitting')) {
    e.stop();
  }
  this.addClassName('submitting').select('.submit').invoke('disable');
  var that = this;
  (function() { that.submit(); }).delay(0.1);
}
```

19 | Providing Input Length Feedback

A common source of frustration when filling in forms is to suddenly see the text input stop dead, even when there was some text warning us of the maximum length. Not only that, but did you know that <textarea> has no maxlength= attribute? Seriously. It's not valid HTML and will be blissfully ignored (unless you're fortunate enough to be able to use HTML5).

So, to provide a unified way to specify maximum lengths, we can rely on dedicated CSS classes for, er, "data storage." They will use a two-part name: first a *maxLength* prefix, then a positive integer, stating the maximum length we want. See the markup on the facing page.

Then we can use JavaScript to do the following:

1. Dynamically decorate the form zones (I'll assume paragraphs, for the sake of brevity) containing these elements (the facing code adds a class to the paragraph), and then dynamically create the placeholder for remaining-length feedback.

2. Initialize the feedback zone to the current state.

3. Bind appropriate event listeners for as-you-type feedback.

4. Position the feedback zone (I put it under the bottom-right corner of its matching field here) and add it to the document, now that it's ready for prime time!

Now whenever typing occurs, we just need to update the feedback, and if we hit or exceed the maximum length (something impossible on a <textarea>), we'll backpedal to the maximum allowed length.

Note a couple of tricks in this code:

- We listen for both *keyup* and *keypress* in order to react to noncharacter keys (deletions, cuts, and pastes, mostly) and character keys. Listening to *keydown* would be useless because it occurs *before* the text changes, and we have no reliable way of determining across browsers and keyboard layouts *whether* the text will change.

- To avoid recomputing the maximum length at every keystroke, we cache it during setup. To associate maximum lengths with our fields, we use a JavaScript-based associative array between the fields' id= attributes[22] and the fields themselves. This is lighter weight than using expando properties.

---

22. We use Prototype's identify( ) here to make sure our element has an id=.

▶ Specify maximum lengths through markup.

form/feedback/index.html

```html
<p>
  <label for="edtDescription">Description</label>
  <textarea id="edtDescription" name="description" cols="40"
   rows="5" class="maxLength200"></textarea>
</p>
```

▶ Set up feedback for maximum-length fields.

form/feedback/feedback.js

```javascript
var maxLengths = {};

function bindMaxLengthFeedbacks() {
  var mlClass, maxLength, feedback;
  $$('*[class^=maxLength]').each(function(field) {
    field.up('p').addClassName('lengthFeedback');
    mlClass = field.className.match(/\bmaxLength(\d+)\b/)[0];
    maxLength = parseInt(mlClass.replace(/\D+/g, ''), 10);

    feedback = new Element('span', { 'class': 'feedback' });
    maxLengths[field.identify()] = [maxLength, feedback];
    updateFeedback(field);
    field.observe('keyup', updateFeedback).
      observe('keypress', updateFeedback);

    feedback.clonePosition(field, { setHeight: false,
      offsetTop: field.offsetHeight + 2 });
    field.insert({ after: feedback });
  });
}
```

▶ Give feedback on the fly.

form/feedback/feedback.js

```javascript
function updateFeedback(e) {
  var field = e.tagName ? e : e.element();
  var current = field.getValue().length,
    data = maxLengths[field.id], max = data[0],
    delta = current < max ? max - current : 0;
  data[1].update('Remaining: ' + delta);
  if (current > max) {
    field.setValue(field.getValue().substring(0, max));
  }
}
```

20 (Un)checking a Whole Set of Checkboxes at Once

It happens time and time again: you have a list, and there are operations your users would like to do *en masse*. The tasks of deleting, moving, archiving, and changing a given property for a number of them all boil down to letting your users check specific items.

And sometimes, all of them. That can be a pain in the butt when the list is long, and that is why *mass toggling* is a nice UI feature.

☐	Subject	Date	From	Size	
☐	Happy new year!	Jan 1, 2010 00:03am	Drew Barrimore	1.6Kb	
☐	What's that great IT book publisher again?	Jan 1, 2010 11:25am	David McClintock	2.3Kb	
☐	You gotta check this out...	Jan 2, 2010 02:15pm	Julianne Moore	4.2Kb	🔗

The markup is simple. Let's just put a checkbox in the table's head section to act as a toggler. This scopes it automatically, letting our script navigate to the matching <tbody> as a container for checkboxes of interest.

The script itself is fairly concise: react to clicks on the toggler by looking up checkboxes in the matching <tbody> and updating their checked= attribute to reflect our togglers.

Now, as an exercise, you could try to adapt this code to achieve two goals:

- Allow multiple tables in the page, with a toggler each. This mostly means you'll replace an id= with a class and use event delegation to avoid registering too many listeners.

- Cater to the more complex tables by allowing *more than one* <tbody> *in a table*. Yes, that is valid markup (one body per semantic section of the table, when you group data in some way). Interestingly, if you add more than one <tbody>, you'll end up *simplifying* the script!

▶ Create the markup for a reference checkbox and a check list.

form/checklist/index_for_book.html

```
<table id="mailbox">
  <thead>
    <tr>
      <th><input type="checkbox" id="toggler" /></th>
      <th>Subject</th>
      <th>Date</th>
      <!-- From, Size, Attachments... -->
    </tr>
  </thead>
  <tbody>
    <tr>
      <td><input type="checkbox" name="mail_ids[]" value="1" /></td>
      <td>Happy new year!</td>
      <td>Jan 1, 2010 00:03am</td>
      <!-- ... -->
    </tr>
    <!-- More rows... -->
  </tbody>
</table>
```

▶ Propagate checked status to first-in-line checkboxes.

form/checklist/checklist.js

```
function toggleAllCheckboxes() {
  var scope = this.up('table').down('tbody'), boxes = scope &&
    scope.select('tr input[type="checkbox"]:first-of-type');
  var refChecked = this.checked;
  (boxes || []).each(function(box) { box.checked = refChecked; });
}

document.observe('dom:loaded', function() {
  $('toggler').observe('click', toggleAllCheckboxes);
});
```

21 Validating Forms: The Basics

Client-side validation is a must-have. Seriously. Regardless of your users' connection throughput, having to do a round-trip on the server for any validations that could be done straight in the browser is a crying shame. You don't want to feel anything but pride about your web pages, so let's dive in!

This first task focuses on the most basic type of validation: required fields, that is, verifying that specific fields have nonblank text or are checked, and so on. We'll use a convention of tagging such fields with the *required* CSS class and rely on styling for visual feedback on missing fields.

First, be sure to intercept the form's *submit* event, not the submit button's *click* or text fields' Return keys. The only surefire way of catching a form before it goes to the server is its *submit* event. It even fires on programmatic submissions (form.submit() calls).

Once hooked in, we just need to grab all elements in the form tagged as *required* and verify that they have a nonblank value. Prototype's blank() extension on String is convenient here. Strings containing nothing but whitespace are deemed blank, and from a semantic point of view, they sure are no better than actual empty strings. Note, however, that if you have a field where whitespace-only is considered all right, you can just use if (field.getValue())—in JavaScript, empty strings are **false**-equivalent.

Our code maintains a firstOffender reference so we can help the user correct input by autofocusing the first problematic field. Last but certainly not least, once we're done with our checks, if there *is* at least one problem, we stop() the event, effectively preventing the current form from being submitted.

As a final reminder, out of the box, *submit* events do not bubble in Internet Explorer. So if your code needs to run in IE too, you would have to attach an event listener for every single form on the page you want to check, including dynamically inserted forms obtained after initial DOM loading. jQuery simulates bubbling for *submit* in IE since version 1.4 but at the cost of somewhat heavy monitoring of all clicks and keypresses within all forms.

▶ Mark required fields.

`form/validation101/index_for_book.html`

```html
<form id="registration">
  <p>
    <label for="user_first_name">First name*</label>
    <input type="text" name="user[first_name]" id="user_first_name"
     class="required text" />
  </p>
  <!-- ...more fields... -->
  <p class="radios">
    <input type="checkbox" id="terms" name="terms" class="required" />
    <label for="terms">I accept the terms of service*</label>
  </p>
  <p><input type="submit" value="Sign me up!" /></p>
</form>
```

▶ Detect missing required fields.

`form/validation101/validation101.js`

```javascript
function checkForm(e) {
  var firstOffender, value;
  this.select('.required').each(function(field) {
    value = field.getValue();
    if (value && !value.blank()) {
      field.up('p').removeClassName('missing');
    } else {
      firstOffender = firstOffender || field;
      field.up('p').addClassName('missing');
    }
  });
  if (firstOffender) { e.stop(); firstOffender.focus(); }
}

document.observe('dom:loaded', function() {
  $('registration').observe('submit', checkForm);
});
```

Related Tasks

- Task 22, *Validating Forms: Going Further*, on the next page
- Task 23, *Validating Forms: The Whole Nine Yards*, on page 60

22 | Validating Forms: Going Further

The previous task had us check that required fields are indeed filled in or checked. Good. However, we'll often want text fields to obey a given format, such as phone numbers, email addresses, integers, or more general numbers. Such fields can be filled in but incorrect, and we should do our best to check that up front. As always, this is a *complement* to the truly mandatory checks, which are the ones on the server side.

The general way to go about this, which is fairly concise and efficient, is a regular expression. Now, if at this point in your developer career you're not comfortable with regular expressions, do yourself a big favor and set aside a couple of hours to dive into them. Although they can look inscrutable to the novice, they are built on very few syntactic rules (about a dozen, half of which are usually sufficient), and knowing "regexes" will save you countless coding hours over and over again. You can find plenty of good, interactive tutorials online.

On the facing page, the idea of the code is to detect CSS classes on form fields that match a regex-based check. I just put three regexes in there, but you can extend features by simply adding new key-value pairs to the FIELD_PATTERNS dictionary. But let me fend off the purists' teeth-grinding right now. Yes, the patterns I show do not cover nondecimal numbers, exponential float notation, and about 0.1 percent of the email addresses in use today. Big deal. But this task is about field validation, not regex-fu. Feel free to tweak the patterns to suit your needs!

This code is fairly short and straightforward; there are just two bits of interest I'd like to shine some light on here. First, the $F(element) function is just a shorthand notation for element.getValue( ).

Second, if you've ever used regexes in JavaScript, odds are you went with the all-purpose myString.match(myPattern) way. This works, because it returns either **null** for no match or an Array of matches (or match groups) otherwise. However, when all you need to know is whether a match was found or not and you don't care about the match's specifics, you should invert the question and ask the pattern to test( ) the String, which just returns a Boolean.

Indeed, the test( ) approach is more robust: it will not break if passed something else than a String, while attempting to call match( ) on a non-String would fail. As an added benefit, test( ) is slightly more efficient. I like to use such bits of performance as a matter of course, especially when they don't carry a code readability (or code weight) penalty.

► Mark fields requiring special syntax.

`form/validation102/index.html`

```html
<p>
  <label for="user_email">Email*</label>
  <input type="text" name="user[email]" id="user_email"
   class="required text email" />
</p>
<p>
  <label for="user_favnumber">Favorite number</label>
  <input type="text" name="user[favnumber]" id="user_favnumber"
   class="text number" />
</p>
```

► Check special-syntax fields.

`form/validation102/validation102.js`

```javascript
var FIELD_PATTERNS = {
  integer: /^\d+$/,
  number: /^\d+(?:\.\d+)?$/,
  email: /^[A-Z0-9._%+-]+@(?:[A-Z0-9-]+\.)+[A-Z]{2,6}$/i
};

function checkField(field) {
  var value = $F(field).toString().strip();
  for (var pattern in FIELD_PATTERNS) {
    if (!field.hasClassName(pattern)) continue;
    if (!FIELD_PATTERNS[pattern].test(value)) return false;
  }
  return true;
}
```

Related Tasks

- Task 21, *Validating Forms: The Basics*, on page 56
- Task 23, *Validating Forms: The Whole Nine Yards*, on the following page

23 Validating Forms: The Whole Nine Yards

The two previous tasks—Task 21, *Validating Forms: The Basics*, on page 56 and Task 22, *Validating Forms: Going Further*, on page 58—dealt with required fields and text input pattern checking. We now need to ping the server side for more up-front checking.

This is our first use of Ajax in this book, an area of JavaScript that can be troublesome to debug. If you haven't yet, read through Appendix B, on page 101, before going on; the information there will, ideally, prove invaluable when you try to troubleshoot or tweak event- or Ajax-driven code.

The poster child of Ajax form validation is unique fields. Most often, this is about logins and email addresses. We'll implement such a check here for a login field, assuming our application mandates having logins that are unique across all users.

An important facet of Ajax validations is on-the-fly UI feedback, with behaviors such as check-in-progress and check-result indicators. So, our markup must plan for these UI elements. On a higher level, you must also decide, perhaps on a per-field basis, what triggering behavior you're looking for. Should you check input *as it's typed* (using high-frequency field monitoring) or *once it's typed* (using *change* events)? In this example, I went with the former option, implying Prototype's Field.Observer mechanism, which I set with a 0.8" interval[23] so as not to strain slow typists too much.

Our check starts by ignoring empty or one-letter inputs, assuming our system requires logins to be at least two characters long (so checks on shorter text would be useless). Then it fires up an Ajax GET request to a server-side checking script and relies on the HTTP response code (2xx = success; anything else is failure, with a special check that status *is* filled in, because Opera ignores many 4xx codes) to update the feedback UI appropriately.

I also put a tiny server-side pseudo-check code in there. It simulates Internet-connection latency so you can see the spinner now and then, and it returns appropriate HTTP response codes, depending on whether the login you typed is already known or not.

---

23. Yes, my geeky friends, I could have said "a 1.25Hz frequency."

▶ Mark up the login field.

form/validation_ajax/index.html

```html
<p>
  <label for="user_login">Login*</label>
  <input type="text" name="user[login]" id="user_login"
   class="required text" />
  <span class="feedback" style="display: none;"></span>
  <img src="spinner.gif" class="spinner" style="display: none;" />
</p>
```

▶ Watch the login.

form/validation_ajax/validation_ajax.js

```javascript
document.observe('dom:loaded', function checkLogin() {
  var feedback = $('user_login').next('.feedback'),
    spinner = $('user_login').next('.spinner');
  new Field.Observer('user_login', 0.8, function(_, value) {
    if (value.length < 2) return;
    feedback.hide(); spinner.show();
    new Ajax.Request('check_login.php', {
      method: 'get', parameters: { login: value },
      onComplete: function(res) {
        if (Ajax.activeRequestCount > 1) return;
        if (res.request.success() && res.status) {
          feedback.update('Login available!').removeClassName('ko');
        } else {
          feedback.update('Login taken!').addClassName('ko');
        }
        spinner.hide(); feedback.show();
      },
    });
  });
});
```

▶ Simulate the login.

form/validation_ajax/check_login.php

```php
<?php
sleep(rand(5, 10) / 10.0); // Simulate intarwebs delay...
$RESERVED = array('bob', 'doudou', 'tdd', 'meshak', 'ook');
$login = isset($_GET['login']) ? $_GET['login'] : '';
$response = in_array($login, $RESERVED) ? '422 Conflict' : '202 Accepted';
header('HTTP/1.1 ' . $response);
?>
```

24 Providing On-the-Fly Help Tooltips on Forms

Sometimes we put complex forms online. Fields have advanced semantics or nontrivial input rules. For instance, we may enforce complexity requirements on password fields, in which case it's best practice (and just plain polite) to warn our users up front. But when multiple fields require detailed warnings and instructions, our forms can get cluttered.

Login*   [_____]   💡 Logins must be unique, at least 3 characters long, and may only use letters, numbers, white space, hyphens, underscores and periods.

Password*   [_____]

First name*   [_____]

Last name*   [_____]

(Sign up)

A useful approach is to put such details in per-field tooltips and make them visible only when needed—when the field has focus. In short, it's a form-related variation on what we did in Task 12, *Pulling Off Classy Tooltips*, on page 34.

Note that the best place for it would be *inside the labels*, not just in the same paragraph. This way, such information is available to, say, blind users regardless of their screen reader's current mode.

Styling—especially in terms of positioning the tooltips—is very important to this task, so I show a bit of CSS on the facing page. But that's admittedly a trivial example. It can be enhanced, both code-wise and performance-wise, if you use a library that simulates bubbling for the *focus* and *blur* events, so you don't have to explicitly register event listeners for every relevant field. At the time of this writing, the latest jQuery does this out of the box, and you'll find more or less official plug-ins for your most popular JavaScript frameworks to fit the same bill.

▶ Put tooltips where they're useful.

form/tooltips/index.html

```
<p>
  <label for="user_login">
    Login*
    <span class="tooltip" style="display: none;">
      Logins must be unique, at least 3 characters long,
      and may only use letters, numbers, white space,
      hyphens, underscores and periods.
    </span>
  </label>
  <input type="text" id="user_login" name="user[login]"
   class="required text" />
</p>
```

▶ Style for uniform, clean appearance.

form/tooltips/tooltips.css

```
#registration label { float: left; width: 6em; position: relative; zoom: 1; }
#registration input.text { width: 14em; }
#registration .tooltip {
  display: block; position: absolute; left: 24em; top: 0;
  padding: 0.35em 0.5em 0.35em 2em; width: 15em;
  border: 1px solid silver;
  color: gray; font-size: 80%;
  background: #ffc url(lightbulb.png) 0.5em 0.3em no-repeat;
}
```

▶ Show on focus, hide on blur.

form/tooltips/tooltips.js

```
document.observe('dom:loaded', function() {
  var attr = Prototype.Browser.IE ? 'htmlFor' : 'for';
  function showTooltip() {
    var tooltip = $$('label['+attr+'="'+this.id+'"] .tooltip').first();
    tooltip && tooltip.show();
  }
  function hideTooltip() {
    var tooltip = $$('label['+attr+'="'+this.id+'"] .tooltip').first();
    tooltip && tooltip.hide();
  }

  $('registration').getInputs().invoke('observe', 'focus', showTooltip).
    invoke('observe', 'blur', hideTooltip);
});
```

25 Autocompleting Input As It's Typed

What's even better than validating input before it's sent to the server? Validating input *as the user types*! By matching users' ongoing input against a database of valid/useful inputs, we can make suggestions that not only help them correct, say, spelling errors, but also save them from manually typing long stuff that is common enough to show up in our suggestions list.

Local search: [_____]

Ajax search: [yan|_____] (capitals of the world)
Georgetown (Guyana)
Naypyidaw (Myanmar)
Pyongyang (North Korea)

This is traditionally referred to as *autocompletion*. The only question is whether your reference datasource is prefetched on the client side (as a simple Array or perhaps a more richly structured object, such as a JSON literal) or is stored on the server, repeatedly queried as typing progresses.

Here's a good rule of thumb: if your datasource is small enough (such as a reference list of states, currencies, or model names within a single brand), prefetch it inside the script (for instance, generate the JavaScript literal for it when rendering the page). Otherwise, go Ajax, and be sure to tune the query frequency so you get good user experience even with slow connections or quick typists.

Script.aculo.us 1.8 has a good autocompletion control with a ton of customization options, which we'll use here, along with its Prototype substrate. Depending on your datasource location, you go with either Autocompleter.Local or Ajax.Autocompleter. (I know, the naming isn't very consistent; sorry about that.) In the first case, you just specify your datasource Array and can tweak match behavior with a handful of options (fullSearch, partialSearch, partialChars, and ignoreCase). In the Ajax case, you provide the base URI and regular Ajax-related options, including extra parameters to send.

▶ Mark up a field for autocompletion.

form/autocompletion/index.html

```
<div class="p" id="local">
  <label for="edtCachedSearch">Local search:</label>
  <input type="text" id="edtCachedSearch" name="search" type="text" />
  <div class="completions"></div>
</div>
```

▶ Style for readability.

form/autocompletion/autocompletion.css

```
.completions {
  border: 1px solid silver; background: white; font-size: 80%; z-index: 2;
}
.completions ul { margin: 0; padding: 0; list-style-type: none; }
.completions li { line-height: 1.5em; white-space: nowrap;
                  overflow: hidden; }
.completions li.selected { background: #ffa; }
.completions strong { color: green; }
```

▶ Autocomplete from a client-side datasource.

form/autocompletion/autocompletion.js

```
var FREQUENT_SEARCHES = [
  'JavaScript', 'JavaScript frameworks', 'Prototype', 'jQuery', 'Dojo',
  'MooTools', 'Ext', 'Ext JS', 'script.aculo.us', 'Scripty2', 'Ajax',
  'XHR', '42'
];

function initLocalCompletions() {
  var field = $('edtCachedSearch'), zone = field.next('.completions');
  new Autocompleter.Local(field, zone, FREQUENT_SEARCHES,
                          { fullSearch: true });
}
```

▶ Autocomplete with Ajax.

form/autocompletion/autocompletion.js

```
function initAjaxCompletions() {
  var field = $('edtAjaxSearch'), zone = field.next('.completions');
  new Ajax.Autocompleter(field, zone, 'autocomplete.php', {
    method: 'get', paramName: 'search' });
}
```

Related Tasks

- Task 23, *Validating Forms: The Whole Nine Yards*, on page 60

26 Using Dynamic Multiple File Uploads

The file upload feature currently built into HTML (as in, pre-HTML5) basically blows. It's single-file, it has no upload progress feedback, it cannot filter on size or file type constraints, and so on. And it uses Base64 encoding, which means every file sent is blown up by 33 percent. Unless we use stuff like WebSockets or SWFUpload, we are stuck with most of these limitations.

However, we *can* improve the user experience a bit by letting users pick multiple files in a nice way. When I say "nice" here, I basically mean "without as many visible file controls as there are files." I like how 37signals presents lists of files-to-be-uploaded in their products: a flat, icon-decorated list of filenames with the option to remove them from the upload "queue."

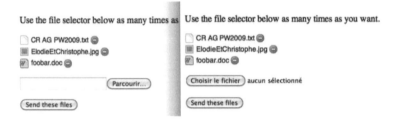

The trick is to clone the file field every time its value is set, move the original file field—hidden—in the "queue," and reset the clone's value so the field appears blank again. The facing code uses a *<ul>* for the queue, synthesizing a *<li>* to hold the file field, filename, and removal icon every time a file is selected. It just feels nicer that way. The next great step would be to exert more control of the input (multiple files at once, size/type constraint enforcement, and so on), but that just isn't possible with the current <input type="file" >; go look up SWFUpload for such nifty features.

The final bit of script shown here gets CSS class names from file extensions using a nice little mapping and handles queue item removal when links in the queue are clicked.

► Create the initial markup for your form.

`form/uploads/index.html`

```html
<form method="post" action="server.php" enctype="multipart/form-data">
  <ul id="uploads"></ul>
  <p><input type="file" name="files[]" id="filSelector" /></p>
  <p><input type="submit" value="Send these files" /></p>
</form>
```

► Queue up file uploads.

`form/uploads/uploads.js`

```javascript
function queueFile() {
  var fileName = $F(this), clone = this.cloneNode(true);
  var item = new Element('li', { 'class': getFileClass(fileName) });
  $(clone).observe('change', queueFile).setValue('');
  this.parentNode.appendChild(clone);
  item.appendChild(this);
  item.appendChild(document.createTextNode(fileName));
  item.insert('<button><img src="remove.png" alt="Remove" /></button>');
  $('uploads').appendChild(item);
}

document.observe('dom:loaded', function() {
  $('filSelector').observe('change', queueFile);
  $('uploads').observe('click', handleQueueRemoval);
});
```

► Add some flair: per-extension styling and queue removal.

`form/uploads/uploads.js`

```javascript
var ICONS = $H({ word: $w('doc docx'), image: $w('jpg jpeg gif png') });

function getFileClass(fileName) {
  var ext = (fileName.match(/\.(.+?)$/) || [])[1].toString().toLowerCase();
  var icon = ICONS.detect(function(pair) { return pair[1].include(ext); });
  return (icon || [])[0];
}

function handleQueueRemoval(e) {
  var trigger = e.findElement('button');
  trigger && trigger.up('li').remove();
}
```

Part V

Talking with the Server Side

The previous part showed us, among other things, how we could go about validating as much input as we could on the client side. It also started dipping into server-provided data for more involved validations, completions, and so on. Most web apps rely on a back end to do their thing; how they "talk" with that back end is the topic of this part.

- We'll first talk about cookies, one of the earliest ways of persisting state across requests, allowing us to create a *session* of navigation for our users so we can remember what they've done, remember who they are, and so on. This is covered in Task 27, *Reading/Writing Cookies*. Permanent cookies, stored on the user's disk, let us "remember" them across visits, too, which can have useful applications. Unfortunately, native cookie manipulation in JavaScript is rather poor; we'll see how to deal with them more easily.

- We'll then focus on the Big Boy of Web 2.0 applications and services: Ajax. First, we'll cover the basics of how to talk with our server without reloading the page; this is in Task 28, *Loading Stuff Through Ajax (Same Domain)*.

- Then we'll get a good look at JSON in Task 29, *Using JSON*, and its cousin JSON-P in Task 30, *Using JSON-P*. These are a great way of exchanging data between a JavaScript-driven client and any server (so much easier to wield than XML).

- Finally, as an opening path toward mashups, we'll cover most of the (numerous) ways of talking with third-party services located on domains other than ours. This is available in Task 31, *Cross-Domain "Ajax" (Take 1)*, and Task 32, *Cross-Domain "Ajax" (Take 2)*.

Debugging Ajax or JSON-P calls can be pretty tricky. If you haven't read through it yet, be sure to check Appendix B, on page 101. You'll get all the tools you need there to comfortably pry into whatever client-server exchanges your code is doing; there's just no point in needlessly wasting hours and pulling your hair.

27 Reading/Writing Cookies

Directly tweaking cookies on the client side is often useful. We can use them to spare our users the need to redefine their settings at every page load by persisting stuff such as pagination size, active tab (in a tabbed UI) across post-and-redirect, collapsed/expanded nodes in a tree, and so on.

Regardless of how we set up these cookies (in scope or expiry), the only native interface to the cookie subsystem we get is the "DOM Level 0" document.cookie property. This property acts as a getter when read and as a setter/deleter when written to. Unfortunately, it didn't go out of its way to provide a neat interface for individual cookie settings. It feels like we're reading and writing raw HTTP headers!

So, to spare us this tedium, most frameworks provide, either directly or through well-known plug-ins, more comfortable access to cookies. Cookie management is a small enough matter, though, that you should not have to depend on a framework for it. Even if you do use a framework already—which you should!—and it has cookie-related features, you may not like its API for it.

That's why, as I show on the facing page, I wrote a stand-alone cookies JavaScript helper. It does not require any framework and attempts to provide a handy API (especially when it comes to options). It's well tested and documented; you may want to give it a shot!

Finally, you should keep in mind a few facts about cookies:

- They reside on the client side, so they're pretty much naked in the wild. You should *never* put sensitive data in there, unless you're encrypting and tamper-proofing them in some robust way.

- They're severely limited in size (4KB) and should therefore not be used for storing large items of data (such as history, complex cart contents, text drafts, and so on).

- They *might not be available*, although this is a very rare phenomenon. What's a bit more frequent, however, is for set-expiry cookies *not to persist across sessions*, because of security policies in the browser (either because of company security policies or because your user configured their browser that way out of privacy concerns).

So, try to use cookies only for extra comfort, especially *persistent* cookies.

▶ Use frameworks or plug-ins.

```
// jQuery Cookies plug-in (http://code.google.com/p/cookies/)
$.cookies.set(key, value[, options])
$.cookies.get(key)
$.cookies.filter(nameRegExp)
$.cookies.del(key[, options])
$.cookies.test()
// MooTools
Cookie.write(key, value[, options])
Cookie.read(key)
Cookie.dispose(key[, options])
// YUI 2 Cookie Utility
YAHOO.util.Cookie.set(name, value[, options]);
YAHOO.util.Cookie.get(name[, typeOrDecoderCallback]);
YAHOO.util.Cookie.remove(name[, options]);
// YUI >= 3
Y.Cookie.set(name, value[, options]);
Y.Cookie.get(name[, typeOrDecoderCallback]);
Y.Cookie.remove(name[, options]);
// Dojo
dojo.cookie(name, value[, options])
dojo.cookie(name)
dojo.cookie(name, null, { expires: -1 });
// Ext
Ext.util.Cookies.set(name, value[, expires][, path][, domain][, secure])
Ext.util.Cookies.get(name)
Ext.util.Cookies.clear(name)
```

▶ Use my stand-alone cookies.js helper.

```
// Helper available at http://github.com/tdd/cookies-js-helper
Cookie.get(name)
Cookie.list([nameRegExp])
Cookie.set(name, value[, options])
Cookie.remove(name[, options])
Cookie.test()
```

28 Loading Stuff Through Ajax (Same Domain)

Performing an Ajax request, especially on the same domain as the current page, is such a fundamental building block of today's web applications that I have to mention how to do it in all major frameworks. However, I could not possibly hope to fit all the details in this one page or even in ten pages. Every framework provides a host of options, settings, and tweaks around Ajax behavior that take a lot of space to cover.

So, I'll just point you in the right direction with the generic signatures on the facing page and provide a few avenues of further exploration:

- All frameworks let you send Ajax requests using any of the four basic HTTP verbs—GET, POST, PUT, and DELETE—and tweaked HTTP headers, so you can interact smoothly with, say, REST services.

- All frameworks provide a number of callbacks—so you can apply custom processing to the Ajax response or pitch in during the request life cycle (start, success/failure, completion, and so on). Common Ajax response formats such as JavaScript, JSON, JSON-P, XML, and HTML often enjoy built-in, automatic decoding (and sometimes automatic processing, especially for JavaScript and JSON-P).

- Several frameworks let you specify general defaults for Ajax options (for instance, jQuery has $.ajaxDefaults) and register global callbacks (commonly used to maintain a single Ajax indicator—such as the famous "spinner"—across all Ajax requests in the page, for example).

- A number of frameworks provide special shortcuts for "Ajaxifying" forms, either using the HTML-mandated serialization for them or letting you tweak it. For instance, YUI 3 has a form option, and Prototype equips <form> elements with a request( ) shortcut.

- Each framework provides a few bits of specific functionality, such as file uploads capability, HTTP basic authentication support, reentrance control and request chaining, response caching, and more.

- You should always make sure to provide useful behavior for both success and failure of your Ajax calls. The failure case is too often ignored or poorly handled.

A final piece of advice: using Ajax requests in *synchronous* mode is roughly equivalent to summoning a vicious demon right in your web page. If you want synchronous, own up to it and just go for a regular page reload!

▶ Make a simple Ajax request.

```
// Prototype
new Ajax.Request(url[, options])
new Ajax.Updater(container, url[, options])
// jQuery
$.ajax([settings])
// MooTools
new Request([options])
// YUI < 3
YAHOO.util.Connect.asyncRequest(method, url, callback, postData)
// YUI >= 3
Y.io(url[, config])
// Dojo
dojo.xhrGet(settings) // or xhrPost, xhrPut, xhrDelete.
// ExtJS
Ext.Ajax.request(settings)
```

▶ Use more involved, Prototype-based features, for a taste.

```
Ajax.Responders.register({
  onCreate: function() { $('spinner').show(); },
  onComplete: function() {
    if (0 == Ajax.activeRequestCount)
      $('spinner').hide();
  }
});

new Ajax.Updater({ success: 'latestUsers' }, '/users/latest', {
  method: 'get',
  parameters: { mode: 'summary', threshold: 'auto' },
  evalScripts: true,
  onFailure: function() {
    logError('We could not fetch the latest logged-in users, sorry.');
  }
});
```

29 | Using JSON

Using JSON has become over the past few years the preferred way of exchanging data between remote resources and JavaScript-based clients. The JSON format[24] is actually a subset of the literal notations allowed by standard JavaScript. JSON has a few limitations but certainly boasts two significant advantages over XML:

- It's more lightweight (less verbose).

- It does not require any particular client-side technology—besides JavaScript itself—to be interpreted and processed.

Nowadays, most server-side technologies provide facilities to encode any eligible data structure into a JSON string and decode such strings when they come in. Depending on your technology of choice, you may need to install an extra library (easily found through Google), but rest assured you're covered with Ruby, PHP, Python, Java, ColdFusion, and ASP.NET, to name but a few.

JSON lets you encode regular, integer-indexed arrays and associative arrays (aka hashes, dictionaries, or maps). In the latter case, keys can be anything (as long as they're quoted), and values can be numbers, strings (barring some escaping), Booleans, **null**, or regular/associative arrays, nested to any depth you need. Decoding it is easy, but producing a JSON string requires some coding, so most JavaScript frameworks do that for you. More often than not, they also provide JSON-specific behavior for Ajax requests, as an extra convenience.

Note that JSON is supposed to be reasonably secure, which is why it doesn't serialize functions. A valid JSON string always boils down to an inert object literal that, when run/interpreted, cannot do any harm by itself. However, if what you get is *not* a valid JSON string—and embeds a malicious function call—you're at risk. This is why most JSON-parsing features offer an option to check/sanitize the string before running it.

This book's code features an example page that fetches a JSON system info object through Ajax and populates a table row with it, using a couple neat tricks. You should check it out!

One of the main ways to use JSON these days is a small trick called JSON-P, which results in passing a JSON object to a callback function predefined in a script. You'll learn more about that in the next task.

---

24. As defined on http://www.json.org/

▶ Decode/encode a JSON string barehanded.

```javascript
// Fast but only as secure as jsonString
var data = eval('(' + jsonString + ')');

// Native JSON support or json2.js; more secure
var data = JSON.parse(jsonString);

JSON.stringify(obj); // Native JSON support
```

▶ Decode/encode a JSON string with frameworks.

```javascript
// Prototype has toJSON() instance methods plus these:
Object.toJSON(obj)
someJsonString.evalJSON([sanitize = false])
// jQuery
$.parseJSON(someJsonString)
// Mootools
JSON.decode(someJsonString[, secure = false])
JSON.encode(obj)
// YUI
Y.JSON.parse(someJsonString)
Y.JSON.stringify(obj)
// Dojo
dojo.fromJson(someJsonString)
dojo.toJson(obj[, prettyPrint = false])
// Ext
Ext.util.JSON.decode(someJsonString)
Ext.util.JSON.encode(obj)
```

Related Tasks

- Task 30, *Using JSON-P*, on the next page

30 Using JSON-P

Using JSON-P is the predominant way to get remote, structured data into a JavaScript-based client. The main transport for it relies on dynamically generated <script> tags, and this has an interesting side effect: *the transport is not restricted by the same-origin policy.* A growing number of web services and APIs (especially the RESTful ones) provide a JSON output format and JSON-P support.

The simple idea behind it is this: you get back a JavaScript source that passes a regular JSON literal to a callback function *you provided*. This means that the callback function was defined beforehand by your own code and made globally available (which is not so great, but we can't work around that).

Now, depending on your mind-set and how much you can trust the remote resources you intend to use with JSON-P, this can be either a relief (this is a great way of emulating cross-domain Ajax) or a concern (JSON-P essentially runs JavaScript generated by a *third-party* in *your page*).

If you're targeting your own server and resources, you're in the clear, and it's all rainbows and unicorns. But if you're targeting third-party resources you do not entirely trust, there could be trouble. Because of the mechanism involved (a <script> tag), you cannot preparse the returned JavaScript to make sure it's a safe JSON-P callback invocation. To get that intermediary step, you'd have to use actual Ajax to get the script, which won't work on all browsers for a third-party resource, as we'll see in the next task.

At any rate, measuring trustworthiness and reliability of your remote JSON-P providers is up to you.

I should point out that the transport we're using—dynamic <script> tags—restricts JSON-P to GET requests and, consecutively, to payloads at about 4KB (a traditional GET limitation). Although there's no magic cure for the latter, with some help from the server side, we can easily turn a GET request into anything else, as we'll see in Task 32, *Cross-Domain "Ajax" (Take 2)*, on page 82.

▶ Implement JSON-P with bare-bones code.

In its simplest form, it just goes like this:

```
server/jsonp/jsonp.js
document.documentElement.firstChild.appendChild(
  new Element('script', { type: 'text/javascript',
    src: this.href + '&r=' + Math.random() }));
```

The previous code executes in the context of a link click handler, so **this** is the <a> element being activated.

The random parameter is there to circumvent browser caching; in production code, you'd check the URI to decide whether to prefix it with & or ?.

A more advanced way is to use dynamic id= attributes for such scripts and remove them post-load to avoid flooding the DOM. The dynamic id= can double as random parameter:

```
server/jsonp/jsonp.js
var script = new Element('script', { type: 'text/javascript',
  src: this.href });
script.src += ('&r=' + script.identify());
script.observe('load', Element.remove.curry(script));
document.documentElement.firstChild.appendChild(script);
```

▶ Use JSON-P facilities from frameworks.

A few frameworks provide functions, specific to JSON-P, that can always come in handy:

```
// jQuery
$.getJSON(url[, data][, callback])
// Mootools
new Request.JSONP({ url: ..., onComplete: function(data) {...} })
// Dojo
dojo.io.script.get({ url: ..., jsonp: function(data) {...} })
```

Related Tasks

• Task 29, *Using JSON*, on page 76
• Task 32, *Cross-Domain "Ajax" (Take 2)*, on page 82

31 | Cross-Domain "Ajax" (Take 1)

Sending data to, or retrieving it from, third-party services is an increasingly common need. In this time of mashups, we routinely need our web pages to communicate with service and content providers, ideally without taxing our own servers in the process.

There are a number of approaches to loading stuff behind the scenes, across domains. I'm going to show you the more important ones and stick to reliable stuff; that should be plenty enough for your actual use cases.

Let me describe the lay of the land real quickly:

- A so-called server-side proxy will work every time, for every URL. If that works for you, you should do it. You might need a number of tweaks if you play with file uploads, content types, POST requests, and the like (always sanitize and check incoming requests, though; you don't want to unwittingly become a spam gateway).

- The future lies with *cross-origin resource sharing* (CORS), the W3C spec for cross-domain requests, which XHR2 uses.[25] Currently, however, this works only on Firefox 3.5+, Safari 4+, and Chrome. IE8 implements the basics (GET only, no custom headers, no credentials, and so on) but requires you to use a custom object, XDomainRequest.

- If both these approaches are unavailable, then your ticket is either JSON-P or dynamic/hidden forms and <*iframe*>s.

- There's no magic bullet for POSTing complex contents to another domain without using a server-side proxy. There are half-solutions (see the next task) but no one-size-fits-all solution.

On the facing page, the book's code for this task illustrates a nice CORS approach (no extra code needed; just use XMLHttpRequest), a server-side proxy approach, and two dynamic approaches based on form and, for one of them, <*iframe*> (one returns a 204 response code, which lets us skip the hidden <*iframe*> target because the browser won't attempt to navigate).

I should stress that you should only bother with forms and <*iframe*>s if you don't want to rely on external services; otherwise, YQL (reviewed in the next task) is definitely your ticket.

---

25. Check out https://developer.mozilla.org/en/HTTP_access_control for more details on CORS and XHR2.

▶ Use a CORS-compliant XMLHttpRequest.

`server/crossdomain1/crossdomain1.js`

```
new Ajax.Updater({ success: 'responses' }, this.href, {
  method: 'get', insertion: 'bottom'
});
```

▶ Use a server-side proxy (from the current domain).

`server/crossdomain1/crossdomain1.js`

```
new Ajax.Updater({ success: 'responses' }, 'ssp.php', {
  method: 'get', parameters: { uri: this.href }, insertion: 'bottom'
});
```

▶ Use a dynamically generated form and *<iframe>*.

`server/crossdomain1/crossdomain1.js`

```
var warp = new Element('iframe', { name: '__blackhole' });
warp.setStyle('width: 0; height: 0; border: 0');
document.body.appendChild(warp);
warp.observe('load', function() {
  $('responses').insert('<p>OK, posted.</p>');
});
var form = new Element('form', { method: 'post', action: this.href,
  target: '__blackhole' });
form.submit();
```

▶ Use a dynamically generated form on a 204 resource.

`server/crossdomain1/crossdomain1.js`

```
var form = new Element('form', { method: 'post', action: this.href });
form.submit();
Element.insert.defer('responses', '<p>OK, posted.</p>');
```

Related Tasks

• Task 32, *Cross-Domain "Ajax" (Take 2)*, on the next page

32 Cross-Domain "Ajax" (Take 2)

There are a few other ways to access other-domain, remote contents behind the scenes. For starters, you can use our trusty JSON-P friend. One interesting use of JSON-P—to access a treasure trove of services, APIs, and contents—is the YQL service by Yahoo! YQL lets you read (and sometimes write to) data tables that map onto just about every possible resource you could dream of: well-known websites and services (search, maps, geolocation, social networks, Flickr, music data, weather, feeds and microformats, and so on). If you haven't played with it yet, head over there *now*.[26]

When it comes to accessing a random resource and returning its raw HTML response, YQL provides two awesome "tables" named *html* and *htmlpost* (the latter one is a *community table* provided by Chris Heilmann and is hence full of win). These let you GET or POST to an HTML-returning resource and will even extract contents for you based on an XPath selector!

I also want to mention a rather nifty approach, dubbed CSSHttpRequest. It does require a server side, though. This relies on the data: URI scheme to embed random contents inside special-name CSS rules. Because CSS files are not subject to the same-origin policy, this works. A small open source library provides the CSSHttpRequest JavaScript object and also server-side code for Ruby, Python, and PHP (which are fairly easy to adapt to other languages). You can get the details online.[27]

The code example for this task in the book's codebase lets you play with all the approaches listed previously.

I'll wrap up with two ways I intentionally didn't include here so you won't say I forgot them. (Ha!) First, you could use a Flash bridge; although this requires some form of CORS information on the server side, there's a library called flXHR that makes this a snap. But Flash is a proprietary technology that I happen to dislike, and even this aside, loading Flash for this is way overkill.

Finally, you could also use a "web bug," a server-side call to a dynamically selected image, through a regular <img> tag (that you would generate with your script). The thing is, the only response you can derive is based on the image dimensions, and properly detecting these after load is, surprisingly, a can of worms. Balancing how limited the response is versus how much jumping-through-flames is required, I avoid this technique.

---

26. http://developer.yahoo.com/yql/
27. http://nb.io/hacks/csshttprequest

▶ Use plain old JSON-P.

```
window.jsonpCallback = function jsonpCallback(data) {
  $('responses').update(data.payload.escapeHTML());
};
document.documentElement.firstChild.appendChild(
  new Element('script', { type: 'text/javascript',
    src: this.href + '?r=' + Math.random() + '&callback=jsonpCallback' }));
```

▶ Use the YQL *html* table with JSON-P-X.

```
function yqlCallback(data) {
  // data.results is an array of matching elements' HTML fragments.
};
var url = "http://github.com/languages/Ruby/updated",
  xpath = "//*[@class='title']",
  yql = 'select * from html where url="'+url+'" and xpath="'+xpath+'"',
  data = { q: yql, format: 'xml', callback: 'yqlCallback' };
document.documentElement.firstChild.appendChild(
  new Element('script', { type: 'text/javascript',
    src: 'http://query.yahooapis.com/v1/public/yql?' +
      Object.toQueryString(data) + '&r=' + Math.random() }));
```

▶ Use the YQL *htmlpost* table with JSON-P.

```
function yqlCallback(data) {
  // data.query.results.postresult.p == array of matching elements' contents.
};
var yql = 'use "http://datatables.org/data/htmlpost.xml" as htmlpost;\
    select * from htmlpost\
    where url="http://demos.pocketjavascript.com/server/jsonp/postdemo.php"\
      and postdata="foo=foo&bar=bar" and xpath="//p"',
    data = { q: yql, format: 'json', callback: 'yqlCallback' };
document.documentElement.firstChild.appendChild(
  new Element('script', { type: 'text/javascript',
    src: 'http://query.yahooapis.com/v1/public/yql?' +
      Object.toQueryString(data) + '&r=' + Math.random() }));
```

▶ Use CSSHttpRequest.

```
CSSHttpRequest.get(this.href, function(res) {
  $('responses').insert('<p>' + res.escapeHTML() + '</p>');
});
```

Related Tasks

- Task 31, *Cross-Domain "Ajax" (Take 1)*, on page 80
- Task 30, *Using JSON-P*, on page 78

Part VI

Making Mashups

The final part of this book covers concrete examples of making your own web page, located on your own domain, talk with third-party services. There won't be any custom server proxy or XML in here, just JSON-P and YQL, so this code is self-contained and works anywhere!

However, you may find only the juicy bits in the code pages of this book. Sometimes a few finishing touches are required to wrap the demo. So, be sure to check these in the source code archive[28] or the live demo site[29] to see how it all fits together.

- Syndicating your Twitter feed on a web page is a common feature nowadays, and doing it on the client side can help when you otherwise heavily cache the hosting page. Task 33, *Syndicating Your Twitter Updates*, has you covered.

- Slapping your recent Flickr photo uploads in a page block somewhere is equally common and is explained in Task 34, *Syndicating Your Flickr Updates*.

- The third task, Task 35, *Geocoding a Location and Getting Photos For It*, explores an increasingly important aspect of the Web: geocoding (not to be confused with geolocation, which is also an important emerging trend but will only work on the latest, bleeding-edge browsers). Essentially, it's about turning place names and addresses into actual geographic coordinates so you can pinpoint them on a map, put them in relation with other data (say, photos from Flickr or tweets!), and create all sorts of useful mashups tying multiple datasets together. The Web and its data are more hackable today than they ever were, and there is enormous potential in what we can do with this!

---

28. http://pragprog.com/titles/pg_js
29. http://demos.pocketjavascript.com/

33 Syndicating Your Twitter Updates

Fetching your recent tweets is a piece of cake, as is using most of Twitter's API. It's just a simple JSON-P call, really!

We won't fetch retweets, mentions, or whatnot here. This is because most Twitter syndication happens in a business context, where your Twitter account is used as an extra marketing channel and you're not interested much in showing retweets, replies, or mentions alongside your own messages. Moreover, the Twitter API does not provide a straightforward way to grab, say, retweets alongside tweets—you'd need two separate calls, one of them authenticated, which means that authentication *to your own account* would be available on the client side *in your visitors' browsers*. And we don't want that. (The other option is syndication on the server side, which falls outside the scope of this book.)

In the code on the facing page, the actual fetching takes only a couple of lines, in the loadTwitterStream( ) method. Twitter gives you read access to any username's direct tweets through a URL,[30] and we're interested in a JSON format here.

What you get back is an array of tweet objects with a wealth of properties, such as created_at, geo, in_reply_to_status_id, source, and text.[31]

The twitterCallback( ) function on the facing page illustrates simple tweet formatting: linking up a reply mention and URLs in general. In the online example code for this task, you'll get an augmented version that also handles hash tags and mentions and shows author information (avatar, name, tweet count, and so on).

Before you do too much with Twitter's API, you should go through Twitter's nice API documentation[32] and also be careful about rate limits enforced on parts of the API to avoid overtaxing the system as your usage scales up.

---

30. http://twitter.com/statuses/user_timeline/username.format
31. You'll get full details at http://apiwiki.twitter.com/Return-Values.
32. http://apiwiki.twitter.com/

▶ Fetch your recent tweets.

The following code relies on Prototype for a few things ($( ), each( ), escapeHTML( ), insert( )...) but is readily convertible to other frameworks.

`mashups/twitter/twitter.js`

```javascript
var REGEXP_URL = new RegExp('(https?://.*?)(\\W?(?:\\s|$))', 'gi');

function twitterCallback(data) {
  var stream = $('twitterStream'), replyTo, contents;
  data.each(function(tweet) {
    contents = tweet.text.escapeHTML().replace(REGEXP_URL,
      '<a href="$1">$1</a>$2');
    if (replyTo = tweet.in_reply_to_screen_name) { // Intentional assign
      contents = contents.replace('@' + replyTo,
        '<a href="http://twitter.com/' + replyTo + '/statuses/' +
        tweet.in_reply_to_status_id + '">$&</a>');
    }
    contents = '<li><p>' + contents + '</p>' +
      '<p class="stamp">' + tweet.created_at + '</p></li>';
    stream.insert(contents);
  });
}

function loadTwitterStream(userName) {
  var uri = 'http://twitter.com/statuses/user_timeline/'+userName+'.json';
  document.documentElement.firstChild.appendChild(
    new Element('script', { type: 'text/javascript',
      src: uri + '?callback=twitterCallback&r=' + Math.random() }));
}
```

▶ Check out part of a JSON-encoded tweet.

(Actual returned datasets are far more detailed, and URLs are obviously not truncated—this is just to give you an idea.)

```
{
  "in_reply_to_screen_name": null,
  "user": {
    "friends_count": 27, "statuses_count": 622,
    "name": "ChristophePorteneuve",
    "followers_count": 215,
    "profile_image_url": "http://a3.twimg.com/.../headshot_tdd_normal.jpg",
  },
  "id": 9537162839, "created_at": "Tue Feb 23 18:35:22 +0000 2010",
  "in_reply_to_status_id": null,
  "text": "15' pour 850m. Sympa av Saint-Ouen + av Clichy aux heures de..."
}
```

34 Syndicating Your Flickr Updates

Flickr provides a fairly large, REST-conformant API, but its useful parts often require authentication, which can be cumbersome and is not, at any rate, very suitable for public-facing syndicated content.

You can get most of the useful query features more easily through YQL. However, in this particular instance, we can just hack through the JSON variant of the Atom feeds Flickr provides for most pages, including user pages. The resulting dataset contains all the information we need, including prebuilt image and profile URLs, dimensions, and publication dates. Such a feed is limited to the latest twenty picture updates, but this remains a great fit for "Flickr updates" syndication.

The JSON fragment on the facing page illustrates the kind of resultset we get. We're mostly interested in the photo thumbnail URL and date of publication here. We could get the original dimensions and date of *taking* with a bit more work, too. However, to keep things simple here, we'll stick to a single request and not too much tweaking.

The image URL we get targets the medium-size version of our photos, when we want smaller, square thumbnails. We just need to change the image URL suffix from _m to _s to fix that.

The facing code also nicely illustrates the Template class from Prototype, which lets us efficiently produce "formatted strings" in a repeatable way.

Again, you can get more information in an unauthenticated way using the YQL tables for Flickr (with one request for the original resultset and then extra queries per photo for further details). And if you need to grab more info yet, or actually update data, the API is there, too.

▶ Fetch someone's public photos.

`mashups/flickr/flickr.js`

```javascript
var FLICKR_ENDPOINT='http://api.flickr.com/services/feeds/photos_public.gne';
var FLICKR_USER_ID ='97027332@N00'; // That's me!
var item = new Template(
  '<li><a href="#{target}"><img src="#{src}" title="#{title}" /></a></li>');


function jsonFlickrFeed(data) {
  var stream = $('flickrStream'), d, dateStr;
  data.items.each(function(photo) {
    d = photo.published.split(/\D/);
    dateStr = d[1] + '/' + d[2] + '/' + d[0];
    stream.insert(item.evaluate({
      src: photo.media.m.replace('_m', '_s'), target: photo.link,
      title: 'Published on ' + dateStr + ' GMT'
    }));
  });
  $('indicator').removeClassName('loading').update('Loaded!');
}


function loadFlickrPhotostream() {
  var uri = FLICKR_ENDPOINT + '?format=json&id=' + FLICKR_USER_ID;
  document.documentElement.firstChild.appendChild(
    new Element('script', { type: 'text/javascript',
      src: uri + '&r=' + Math.random() }));
}
```

▶ Check out some of the JSON-P response.

```javascript
jsonFlickrFeed({
  // ...
  "items": [
  {
   "title": "P1010071",
   "link": "http://www.flickr.com/photos/97027332@N00/4105961623/",
   "media": {
     "m":"http://farm3.static.flickr.com/2638/4105961623_ec0ca9c164_m.jpg"
   },
   "date_taken": "2009-11-12T15:38:21-08:00",
   // ...
   "published": "2009-11-15T18:54:21Z",
   // ...
  },
  // ...
  ]
})
```

35 Geocoding a Location and Getting Photos For It

Geolocation has become a very common need, mostly thanks to the rise of the mobile Web, so we're going to illustrate the two main aspects of it:

- First, turning a textual location (address, city, region or state, country) into a geolocation (which essentially boils down to a latitude and a longitude)[33]

- Second, searching data based on these geocoordinates

A lot of APIs are available, including prominent "geocoders" from Google, Yahoo!, Geonames, and others. For our purposes, I'll use a very simple, straightforward, and useful tool: Yahoo's Placemaker API and Christian Heilmann's JavaScript wrapper for it, JS-Placemaker. This API lets us analyze any text to extract one or more potential geolocations for it, and we'll use that to turn a location name (say, something typed into a form field) into latitude and longitude coordinates.

Like all Yahoo! Developer Network APIs, Placemaker requires a Yahoo! AppID; the sample code on the facing page includes a working one, but you should get your own AppIDs to play with.[34] Then all you need to do is provide the JavaScript wrapper with it and call its getPlaces( ) method with the text to analyze, a callback to process the results, and optionally the text's locale (for instance, *en-US* or *fr-FR*) to help Placemaker analyze it correctly.

Notice a tiny trick in the code to "normalize" the resultset toward a guaranteed array of places. Because a one-match case has a single match property and a multiple-match case returns an array named matches, we use a (matches || [match]) construct to access both situations as an array.

On the Flickr side of things, we just use the *flickr.photos.search* method with its geo-related parameters lat and lon, through a JSON-P call very much like in the previous task. Because we're doing a global search here, we don't need to specify a user ID this time.

If you're interested in georelated tricks and hacks that are on the client side and JavaScript-based—including GeoIP and the W3C Geo API—you can find a wealth of info, demos, and cool stuff on the page maintained by evangelist extraordinaire Christian Heilmann.[35]

---

33. Often you'll also want to use extra data such as accuracy and the resulting bounding box.
34. Get those at https://developer.apps.yahoo.com/wsregapp/.
35. http://isithackday.com/hacks/geo/

▶ Fetch geolocations for any given text.

(The following code actually assumes only the first resulting geolocation is relevant.)

`mashups/geo/geo.js`

```javascript
// Use your *own* API key for your own code :-)
var YAHOO_APPID = 'KwWEZW_V34GVYNWWOLZm6NT.' +
  'XfIwNrF9ysko8qu6sDuE6SbehuptUZQp6jKF130V25hFTMrrdrbQeo4-';

function getGeoLocationFor(text) {
  Placemaker.config.appID = YAHOO_APPID;
  $('indicator').addClassName('loading').update('Getting geolocation for ' +
    text.escapeHTML() + '...').show();
  Placemaker.getPlaces(text, function(places) {
    if (places.error) {
      $('indicator').removeClassName('loading').
        update(places.error.escapeHTML());
    } else {
      var loc = (places.matches || [places.match])[0].place;
      $('indicator').update('Loading ' + loc.name +
        ' pics (' + loc.type + ')...');
      getGeoPhotos(loc.centroid.latitude, loc.centroid.longitude);
    }
  }, 'en-US');
}
```

▶ Fetch geolocated photos from Flickr.

`mashups/geo/geo.js`

```javascript
// flickrCallback is very similar to the Flickr syndication task's code.
// Get full example code at http://pragprog.com/titles/pg_js/source_code

function getGeoPhotos(lat, lon) {
  $('indicator').addClassName('loading').show();
  var uri = FLICKR_ENDPOINT + '?' + Object.toQueryString({
    method: 'flickr.photos.search', api_key: FLICKR_API_KEY,
    extras: 'date_taken,url_sq,description', lat: lat, lon: lon,
    per_page: 50, format: 'json', jsoncallback: 'flickrCallback'
  });
  document.documentElement.firstChild.appendChild(
    new Element('script', { type: 'text/javascript',
      src: uri + '&amp;r=' + Math.random() }));
}
```

Part VII

Appendices

JavaScript Cheat Sheet

JavaScript Cheat Sheet

Intentionally not exhaustive, but with all the choiciest bits and plenty of advice and tips. v1.0.

Built-in types & literals

Number	0, 42, 0.15, 3e10, -3.12e-2
String	"Hello", 'hello' (both allow escapes) Common escapes: \r \n \t \" \' \uXXXX (hex) \0oo (octal)
Boolean	true, false
Array	[], [1, 2, 3], [[[3], 2], 1]…
Date	new Date(…) (no literal notation)
RegExp	/pattern/flags (see dedicated pad)
Function	function(…) {…} (see dedicated pad)
Object	{ prop: value, prop2: value2… }

typeof *expression* → type name, lower-cased

Boolean conversions: 0, '' (empty string), null and undefined are deemed false. Everything else is considered true.

Regular expression redux

Classes (sets of matching characters)	. \d \D \w \W \s \S […] [^…] (literal hyphen must be at end)
Boundaries	\A \Z ^ $ \b \B
Greedy quantifiers (largest match)	* (0+) ? (0-1) + (1+) {min,} {,max} {min,max}
Reluctant quantifiers (smallest match)	*? ?? +?
Grouping	(…) captures (back-ref'able), (?:…) doesn't capture (faster)
Look-aheads	(?=…) requires a match, (?!…) requires a nonmatch
Back-references	\1…\9 (captures groups), \& (entire match)
Alternative	│ (if inside a group, limited to it)

Flags:

g	Global: matches not just the first occurrence, but all of them.
i	Case-insensitive (Unicode-aware, too!)
m	Multiline: the dot class (.) matches any character, *including line breaks*

- Compiling a regex again and again is slow: pre-compile in a constant.
- If you just need to test whether there is a match but don't care about the details (groups, etc.), use regex.test(str) instead of str.match(regex).
- If you don't need to capture a group for later reference, but just need to apply a quantifier to a group, mark the group as non-captured: (?:…).

Functions

- Declaration: function fxName(…) { … }
- Expression: function(…) { … }

Declarations are "hoisted" within their scope: any of them can use any other one, regardless of their order (no "prototype declarations" needed).

- "return x;" exits the function with return value x.
- "return;" exits with return value undefined.

Functions are objects like any other, so they have methods of their own (e.g. apply, call) and can be passed around by reference (but you'll lose their binding: their original meaning for the "this" keyword.). This means you can assign them to variables and pass them as arguments, for instance.

Argument lists don't specify types, and just serve as "hints" that auto-assign names to the first few actual arguments passed. But any JS function is "varargs": you can pass as many arguments as you want, and access them through the built-in arguments variable, which behaves quite like an Array (it has length and []).

Special values

undefined	variable with no value yet, parameter with no matching argument passed.
null	not quite undefined; often the value of a "no result" DOM call, and a way to programmatically assign "no value" to something.
false, true	the two boolean literals.
Infinity	Numeric infinity (can be signed, e.g. -Infinity).
NaN	Result of a Not-a-Number expression, such as a failed number parse. Not equal to any numeric, including itself. Use isNaN(n) for proper detection.

Operators

Arithmetics: + - * / % ++ --

Remember: there's no int/float, just Numbers!
- % = modulo/remainder. Unary minus inverts sign: -42.
- ++ and -- increment/decrement. Unless there's a clear reason to use them as suffixes (x++), **favor prefixes** (++x).

Comparisons: == === < > <= >= !=

- == only compares values, using "conversion protocols." So 5 == "5", 0 == false, null == undefined…
- === does *strict comparison*: value + type. Great for testing undefined ===
- != means not-equal-to (like VB/SQL's <>).

Boolean logic: && (and) || (or)

Just remember:
- && has priority over ||
- a || b short-circuits (doesn't evaluate) b if a (…converts to true)
- a && b short-circuits b unless a

Arithmetics shorthands: += -= *= /= %=

a += b behaves like a = a + b, and so on. More concise!

Member selection: […]

- Array selection by index: array[5] (starts at 0).
- Dynamic member selection:
  - obj['propName'] ⇔ obj.propName
  - obj['methodName'](…) ⇔ obj.methodName(…)
    e.g. node[visible ? 'show' : 'hide']();

Priorities: mostly like C/C++/Java/Ruby's…

- * / % over + -
- && over ||
- (…) forces priority
(5 * 3) + (6 / 2) ⇔ 5 * 3 + 6 / 2
(a && b) || (c && d) ⇔ a && b || c && d

Bitwise ops (rarely needed): & | ^ << >> >>>

^ is a XOR, << and >> shift bits (>>> with sign loss / zero-filling)

Variables and scopes

var x, y = 42, z, t = y * 2;

Local variables must be declared using **var**.
You should strive not to use/leak global variables.

Variables can be assigned on-the-fly at declaration. They're accessible from anywhere in their containing scope (mostly means: the current function).

If your code nees to hide some of its identifiers, be they variables or functions, use the **module pattern:**

```
(function() {
    // what's in here stays in here unless you explicitly
    // bring it out by return or direct assignment.
})();
```

Deciding what path to take

```
if (condition) {                switch (expr) {
    code                            case valueA:
}                                       codeA
                                        break;
if (condA) {                        case valB1:
    codeA                           case valB2:
} else if (condB) {                     codeB
    codeB                               break;
} else {                            default:
    codeC                               codeC
}                               }
```

Protip: early tests with returning code let you avoid nesting the rest in an `else` block and keep your indentation sane!

Array stuff you should know

```
var arr = [2, 3, 4, 5, 6];

arr.length              // => 5
arr.concat([7, 8, 9])   // => [2..9]
arr                     // => [2..9]
arr.push(10)            // => [2..10]
arr.unshift(1)          // => [1..10]
arr.pop()               // => 10
arr.shift()             // => 1
arr                     // => [2..9]
arr.slice(4, -2)        // => [6, 7, 8]
arr.join('')            // => '23456789'

arr.sort(function(a, b) {
    return b - a;
}) // => [9, 8, 7, 6, 5, 4, 3, 2]

arr.sort()    // => [2, 3, 4, 5, 6, 7, 8, 9]
arr.splice(5) // => [7, 8, 9]
arr           // => [2, 3, 4, 5, 6]
```

Exception/error handling

```
try {
    thisCodeMayExplode
} catch(e) {
    thisCodeRunsOnlyOnErrors // e refers to the error object
} finally {
    thisCodeRunsWhetherOrNotThereIsAnError
}
```

You can raise your own errors (any object will do) with `raise exceptionObject`.

Math functions

The global Math object is replete with static methods for all the common operations, and a number of useful constants. Here's a sample:

- Powers: E LN2 LN10 LOG2E LOG10E SQRT1_2 SQRT2 exp log pow sqrt
- Trigonometry: PI acos asin atan atan2 cos sin tan
- Rounding/misc: abs ceil floor max min random round

Asynchronous code: using timeouts

```
var timer;
function callback() {
    timer && window.clearTimeout(timer);
    timer = null;
    callbackCode;
}

window.setTimeout(callback, 100); // 0.1 second
```

Poor man's debugger

The global/window object has `alert(...)`, which lets you popup a message box. Whenever possible (Safari, Firefox with Firebug, Opera, IE8+) use a console facility for an easier debugging experience.

Firebug's `console` object has a whole lot more to it than `console.log`: check http://getfirebug.com/logging.

Looping around

```
for (decl; test; incr) {        while (cond) {
    code                            codePerhapsNeverRun
}                               }

do {                            while (true) {
    codeRunAtLeastOnce              codeRunAtLeastOnce
} while (cond)                      if (skipRestOfTurn)
                                        continue;
                                    if (justStopLooping)
"Fast array loop":                      break;
                                    remainderCode
                                }
for (var i = 0, l = arr.length; i < l; ++i)
    code
```

Really useful String stuff

First, there's a `length` property (characters, not bytes).

```
'yay'.charAt(1)              // => 'a'
'hello'.indexOf('l')         // => 2
'hello'.indexOf('l', 3)      // => 3 (specified min pos)
'hello'.lastIndexOf('l')     // => 3
'hello'.lastIndexOf('l', 2)  // => 2 (specified max pos)
'hello'.replace('l', 'L')    // => 'heLlo'
'hello'.replace(/[aeiouy]/g, '-') // => 'h-ll-'

'hello'.replace(/(.)\1/g, function(s) {
    return s.toUpperCase();
}) // => 'heLLo'

'a b c'.split(' ')       // => ['a', 'b', 'c']
'a b \nc'.split(/\s+/)   // => ['a', 'b', 'c']
'abc'.split('')          // => ['a', 'b', 'c']
'a b c'.split(' ', 2)    // => ['a', 'bc'] (specific max count)
'hello'.substring(2)     // => 'llo'
'hello'.substring(2, 4)  // => 'll' (specified end boundary)
'hello'.slice(-3)        // => 'llo' (start 3 from end)
'hello'.slice(-3, -1)    // => 'll' (specified end boundary, 2 from end)
'ÉlodiE'.toLowerCase()   // => 'élodie'
'déjà ça'.toUpperCase()  // => 'DÉJÀ ÇA'
'hello'.match(/(.)\1/)   // => ['ll', 'l'] †
```

† full match at index 0, captured group 1 at index 1, etc.

A few global goodies

```
var x = 5;
eval('x * Math.sqrt(16)')            // => 20 – Handle with care!
decodeURIComponent('%C3%89lodie')    // => 'Élodie'
encodeURIComponent('S & H')          // => 'S%20%26%20H'
parseInt('010')                      // => 8 †
parseInt('08')                       // => NaN †
parseInt('010', 10)                  // => 10 ‡
parseFloat('314.15e-2')              // => 3.1415
isNaN(parseInt('foobar'))            // => true
Math.PI.toFixed(3)                   // => 3.142
(5.31762).toFixed(3)                 // => 5.318
Math.PI.toPrecision(3)               // => 3.14
```

† without an explicit radix, parseInt auto-detects. A 0 prefix hints at octal, so…
‡ with an explicit radix, no possible confusion. This is the preferred calling form.

Identifiers and reserved words

Identifiers must start with $, _ or a Unicode letter (still, you should refrain from using identifiers in, say, Aramaic!), and may continue with any of this plus Unicode digits.

There are no less than 56 reserved words, most of which are not actual keywords in current versions of JavaScript:

```
abstract boolean break byte case catch char class const continue
debugger default delete do double else enum export extends final
finally float for function goto if implements import in instanceof
int interface long native new package private protected public
return short static super switch synchronized this throw throws
transient try typeof var void volatile while with
```

Debugging JavaScript

B.1 Here Be Dragons

Just a few years back, the art of debugging JavaScript code felt like handling unstable nitroglycerine blindfolded on a trampoline. Not only did we feel dramatically under-equipped, but the few tools we did have at our disposal were rather unwieldy and on the whole did not feel very helpful (except, in all fairness, for the IE debugging tools inside Visual Web Developer Express, which had been there for a while and were quite good).

After all, JavaScript debugging at the time seemed so borderline dangerous that, in its time-honored Ghostbusters-based code name tradition, Mozilla's JavaScript debugger was christened Venkman, and its baseline was "Don't cross the streams." Yes, things were—or at least felt—that hazardous.

Then Joe Hewitt dropped by and released to the world what he unassumingly referred to as "just a bunch of scripts put together." Firebug cast a great beacon of light on our forsaken field (that is, front-end web development), and there was much rejoicing in the land.

And because the bar had been so raised and the game so changed, good people from all browser vendors rolled up their sleeves and started tackling these problems again, in their own ways, which is why we now have Safari's Web Inspector, Opera's Dragonfly, and, yes, even a pretty decent JavaScript debugger in Internet Explorer 8. Still, Firebug keeps plowing ahead (at somewhat varying speed, admittedly) and retains a special place in the hearts of web developers.

Setting Up a Debug Bench

The walk-throughs in this appendix all use a test page with a bit of JavaScript to step through, play with, and generally demo the script-debugging facilities of each browser. You can find these two files—debugbench.html and its debugbench.js dependency—in the online code archive for this book.

Here's the HTML page, which is as bare-bones as it gets:

debugbench.html

```
<!DOCTYPE html PUBLIC "-//W3C//DTD XHTML 1.0 Strict//EN"
  "http://www.w3.org/TR/xhtml1/DTD/xhtml1-strict.dtd">
<html>
<head>
  <meta http-equiv="Content-Type" content="text/html; charset=UTF-8" />
  <script type="text/javascript" src="debugbench.js"></script>
  <title>Pocket JavaScript debug bench</title>
</head>
<body>
  <h1>Debug bench</h1>
  <input type="button" onclick="alert(fibo(20))" value="Fibo(20)" />
</body>
</html>
```

And here's the JavaScript source we'll play with:

debugbench.js

```
function fibo(base) {
  if (base <= 2)
    return 1;
  return fibo(base - 1) + fibo(base - 2);
}
```

B.2 Firefox and Firebug

You can grab Firebug at http://getfirebug.comor from the Mozilla Add-Ons directory at http://addons.mozilla.org. At the time of this writing, Firebug is ramping up to release its 1.4 version; several alphas having been around for a while. Firebug had a somewhat difficult period for a while, when its Ajax-related features resulted in weird behaviors such as double requests, but it's been mending and is coming back to us in better shape than ever. So, if you left it during the 1.2 to 1.3 era, you should definitely give it another try.

By default, Firebug's features are disabled on any address you're browsing, including local files. This is for performance reasons, and you just need to click the bug icon on the right side of your status bar to open the Firebug panel and start enabling the features you want for the current domain, page, or file.

Firebug is very feature-rich, but the areas of most concern for this book are the Console and Script tabs. The console is a live JavaScript command line and a log area your scripts can write to using the global console object and its built-in methods such as log( ), debug( ), error( ), and group( ), to name but a few. (Read about the whole console API on Firebug's website.)

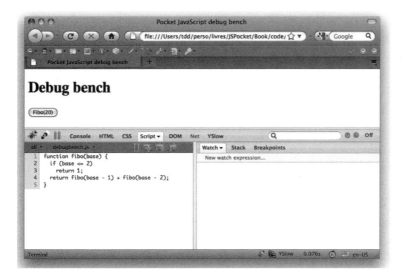

Figure B.1: FIREBUG'S BASIC SCRIPT VIEW ON OUR DEBUG BENCH

The Script tab is the actual debugger. It lets you browse all the JavaScript parts of your page (loaded files, inline event attributes, and so on), set breakpoints, step through your code, keep an eye on specific expressions or variables (on the Watch subtab), and look at the current stack trace (in the Stack subtab). It's all we need for scrutinizing our JavaScript code as it runs.

The basic view of the script debugger for our test bench is shown in Figure B.1.

There are basically two ways to get code running here: either drop into the console and type away JavaScript that triggers the code we intend to examine or cause events in the page that trigger the same code.[1] In our debug bench page, our fibo( ) function is called with argument 20 when a button is pressed. You can verify this works by clicking the button—you should get a dialog box with the result (6,765). There are a number of things you can do in the debugger to dig into the details of this function's execution:

- Choose a script file (or HTML page with inline scripts): click the arrow next to the filename above the source pane, and select your file.

---

1. Technically, many debuggers let you get into step-by-step mode any time an exception is raised (that is, when an error happens). In Firebug, click the arrow next to the Script tab's label for this kind of feature.

- Toggle breakpoints on specific lines of code: just click at the line's level in the source pane's left gutter.

- Require that a given condition be satisfied for a breakpoint to trigger: right-click the breakpoint's bullet in the gutter, and type the JavaScript expression for the condition.

- Disable a breakpoint for a while, without losing its position and conditions: go to the Breakpoints subtab, and uncheck the breakpoint's checkbox.

- Once a breakpoint was hit, step through the code: icons above the source pane let you step into (that is, if the current line calls a function, step inside that function), step over (just run such function calls without stepping inside them), and step out (run the current function and resume manual stepping once back in the caller function).

- At any time, keep an eye on local variables and values for any expression of interest you would have set up earlier: just look into the Watch subtab.

We'll go through a number of these steps manually here as an example manipulation you can reproduce on the other browsers, to get a hang of things. First, let's say we want to get into step-by-step mode when the fibo( ) function is called with an argument that's small enough—say, less than 5. To do this, we first need to set the breakpoint on the function's first line and then equip that breakpoint with the appropriate condition.

1. Click in the source pane's gutter, facing the function's first line (line 2).

2. Right-click the red dot that appeared to signal the breakpoint's presence, and type the condition you need in the tooltip: base < 5. You should see something similar to Figure B.2, on the next page. Validate.

You're all set! Now click the Fibo(20) button in the web page; the function will start its recursive descent, and you should hit the breakpoint. Click the Stack subtab in the right pane to see where you're at; you should see something like Figure B.3, on the facing page, which lets you see the current state of recursion: 15 levels down already (if you scroll down, you'll see the initial onclick= handler call).

By clicking the Watch subtab, you can see all the local variables, including the current *binding* (what object **this** is currently referencing) and arguments. In Figure B.4, on page 106, you can see that we're running as a global function (**this** currently references the global window object) and the base argument

Figure B.2: SETTING A CONDITIONAL BREAKPOINT IN FIREBUG

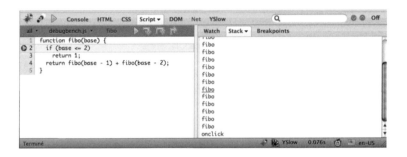

Figure B.3: A STACK TRACE VIEW IN FIREBUG

is 4. Note that you could also use the Watch subtab to *change* these values by just double-clicking the value line in the list and typing the new value.

Let's explore the various kinds of stepping now. You should be on the fibo( ) function's first inner line (line 2) just now. Click the Step Into icon (the one immediately to the right of the blue Play icon used to resume execution) once. Since the condition is false, the next line is skipped, and you get to the **return** line. Hit the same icon again. Since it's a function call and you're stepping *into*, you'll get one level down and recurse your way into the same function, this time with base being 3 (glance at the Watch subtab to verify this).

Let's say you're not interested in digging any deeper now, and you just want to run the code until you're back at the level you just left (base equal to 4). To do this, follow these steps:

1. You'll first need to remove, or at least disable, the breakpoint you set earlier. Otherwise, it'll keep breaking your stride any time the code

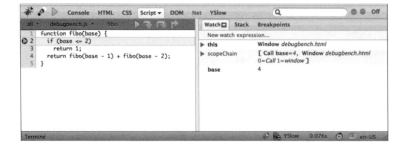

Figure B.4: THE WATCH VIEW IN FIREBUG

calls fibo( ) with an argument less than 5. Click over to the Breakpoints subtab, and uncheck your breakpoint to disable it.

2. Then click the Step Out icon (the last one above the source pane) to let the code run away until it hits the previous stack trace level again. You should find yourself on the **return** line you had come from, with base being equal to 4 again.

3. Repeating that operation will have you run back up the trace again and again (meaning the base watch is tracing back to values higher and higher), so that after a short while, you'll notice the stack trace on the right is thinning up on the Stack subtab.

4. When you're tired of manually stepping and want to just resume normal execution, hit the Play button (the blue right arrow).

Note that all these stepping/running icons have shortcut keys, but these vary widely based on the platform you're running Firebug on. They're usually mentioned in the icons' tooltips, so just let your mouse hover on them to figure out these shortcuts.

B.3 Safari and Web Inspector

Safari has been honing its Web Inspector in recent years, and version 4.0 comes with a very decent feature set. (I hear current "nightlies" are making really good progress, too.) Although it is currently a bit subpar (with regard to Firebug) when it comes to DOM modification, its console and JavaScript debugger are certainly equivalent.

The Web Inspector's Scripts section, with its console pane open, is shown in Figure B.5, on the facing page (you can use one of the bottom-row icons

Figure B.5: SAFARI'S WEB INSPECTOR

Figure B.6: STEPPING IN WEB INSPECTOR

or simply the [Esc] key to toggle the console on and off, regardless of your currently visible section).

In the current public release of Safari, Web Inspector differs from Firebug in a few key places; for instance, you cannot exactly remove a breakpoint. You can only disable it. You cannot put a condition to it, either. And there are no watches. Still, it's already a pretty useful tool (and upcoming releases only get better). You can see what stepping looks like a few levels down in the recursion stack, as shown in Figure B.6, which shows how similar its behavior is to Firebug's.

B.4 IE6, IE7, the IE Toolbar, and Web Developer Express

Internet Explorer has long been the bane of web developers, if only because of its sudden development halt once the "browser wars" were over and Netscape lay dead on the field. Microsoft is putting some significant effort now into recent versions of Internet Explorer (IE8 and IE9 typically make great leaps forward), but IE6 and IE7 are more than a decade behind the competition when it comes to web standards, including JavaScript support.

To add insult to injury, there is not even a remotely decent JavaScript debugger built into these browsers. There's a rather dumb error console, and that's it. When scouting around for debugging solutions applicable to these either of these versions, you'll find a few options.

Leaving aside the antiquated Microsoft Script Debugger, the most common tool is the *Visual Web Developer Express edition*: This is the free, limited edition of Microsoft's mammoth Visual Web Developer tool, which is really a customized version of its Visual Studio series, targeted at web developers. It's been around for a while and has a rather good JavaScript debugger.

So yes, unless you already use such tools for development (say, you do .NET stuff), you would have to download a multigigabyte file (the installer, at 2.6MB, is just a proxy tool) just to debug JavaScript. But if you need to debug JavaScript in IE6 or IE7, it is worth going through, if only to preserve your sanity.[2] When configuring, remember that neither Silverlight nor SQL Server are quite necessary for our purpose here.

Once installed, launch Visual Web Developer Express edition (that's quite a mouthful, so let's just say "VWDE" from now on, shall we?); once it completes initial setup, you'll get a welcome page similar to Figure B.7, on the facing page.

The Express edition, being free, tries to reduce our elbow room by not letting us attach to a running browser. The trick, then, is to use it to *spawn* an *attached browser*. This is a web browser spawned by VWDE in debug mode, so any JavaScript errors get intercepted by VWDE's debugger.

Once we have an attached browser, we can use it to surf wherever we please. Errors will drop us right into the debugger, and we can also grab running documents inside VWDE and put breakpoints and such in them. To replicate the manipulations from the first section of this appendix, you'll need the latter option.

To spawn an attached IE6 or IE7 browser, we need to play ball a bit with VWDE's requirements.

---

2. You can download it at http://www.microsoft.com/express/download/default.aspx.

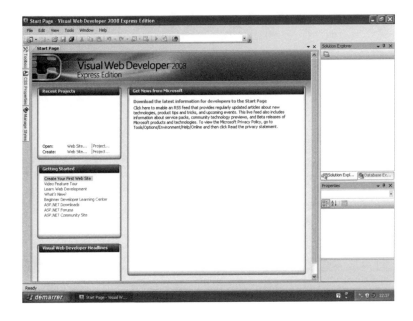

Figure B.7: Visual Web Developer 2008 Express edition: Welcome

There are essentially two rules we must abide by here:

- We must have a VWDE *project* set up and with debugging enabled.

- We must set IE7 as our default browser so that it is the one launched by the "Start debugging" feature.

Both requirements need only be dealt with once (unless you're testing this on the machine where you also surf on a regular basis and therefore need to switch your default browser back and forth between IE and whatever elected browser you have). Let's address these requirements:

1. Open IE6 or IE7, and click Tools > Internet Options....

2. Go to the Advanced tab, and scroll to the Browsing section.

3. Make sure "Display a notification about every script error" is checked and both "Disable script debugging..." are *unchecked*.

4. Close IE entirely.

5. Click File > New Web Site....

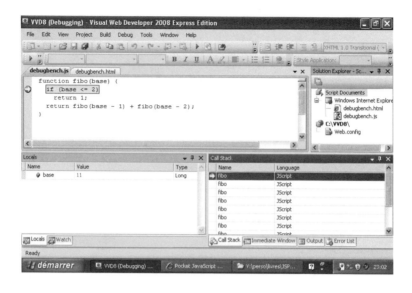

Figure B.8: DEBUGGING IE7 WITH BREAKPOINTS

6. Select the Empty Web Site option, and browse to whatever dummy directory you want to set it up in. Click OK.

7. Click the "Start debugging" menu option or icon (the green arrow).

8. This first time around, VWDE detects your project is not yet set up for debugging. It lacks a special Web.config file. A dialog box offers to create it for you or continue without debugging—obviously, leave the first option checked, and click OK.

9. You should see a development server on a dynamic port started in the taskbar, and your IE opens up on an empty directory listing named after your project's directory (a warning bar may tell you the browser is working using the Intranet security zone, which is fine with us). *You're set to go!*

Now that we're all set up, just browse to our debugbench.html file any which way. Once opened, look into VWDE. On the right, in the Solution Explorer panel, you should see a Running documents branch with debugbench.html and debugbench.js listed. Double-click the latter.

You're there! You can now set your breakpoint on line 2 the usual way (click in the gutter), switch back to your IE, and click the Fibo(20) button. You drop back to the debugger in stepping mode, as shown in Figure B.8. *Voila!*

B.5   IE8 and Developer Tools

There's no question about it: Internet Explorer 8 is a great step forward in the IE world. Aside from the notable improvements in web standards support (although it still lags far behind modern browsers, it's certainly not stuck in the Cretaceous anymore), these points are of immediate interest to us Java-Scripters:

- The JScript engine in IE8 is on average seven times slower than other JavaScript engines in released browsers. This peaks at a factor of almost twelve against Chrome's v8 or the latest builds of Safari's Squirrelfish Extreme and Firefox's Tracemonkey.

  Why is that a good news? IE7 used to be up to *ninety times* slower. And IE6 couldn't live with the shame of its own factor figure. So, the IE team managed to improve its JScript engine by a factor of about thirteen, which has to be declared awesome, like it or not.

- The DOM performance in IE8, which is our second major pain point when scripting, has also received some significant love and is now lagging by an average factor of "only" four, which is also a major improvement.

- IE8 has built-in "Developer Tools," which are a cleaned-up, snappier version of the IE Developer Toolbar we use in IE6 and IE7, with an actual *JavaScript debugger* thrown in. One that actually works and doesn't entail incessant glitches between IE and an external debugging app.

So, not only can we start thinking about reenabling our fancy effects and Ajax operations in the IE world, but we can also do so knowing debugging got a whole lot easier!

Incidentally, IE8 also explores ways to reduce the perceived performance impact of script loading. You still should use generic optimizations such as "load scripts at the bottom of the "[3] and, even more importantly, script concatenation (for example, through Sprockets[4]) and gzip'ping.[5]

The IE8 Developer Tools pane with its Script tab opened and a debugging session going on is shown in Figure B.9, on the following page, with our now-familiar breakpoint. Toggling the debugger on and off is simply a matter of clicking the large button in the toolbar, and we get the usual stepping

---

3.   http://developer.yahoo.com/performance/rules.html#js_bottom
4.   http://getsprockets.com
5.   For lots of great advice about web page loading and rendering performance, get Thomas Fuchs and Amy Hoy's excellent *JavaScript Performance Rocks!* [HF09], and check out the Performance tips on the Yahoo! Developer Network at http://developer.yahoo.com/performance/rules.html.

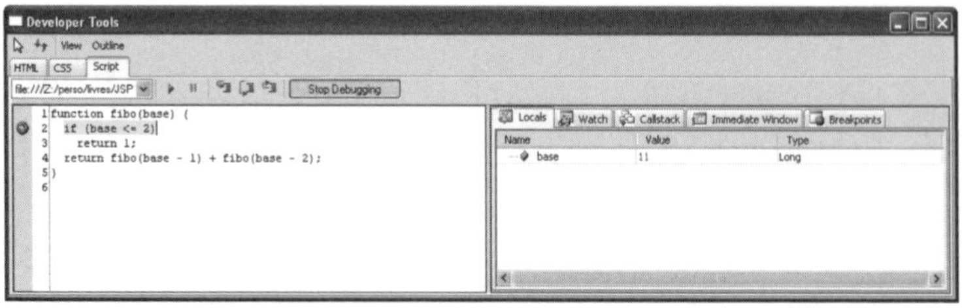

Figure B.9: IE8 DEVELOPER TOOLS: SCRIPT TAB

options, local variables, watches, callstack inspection, a sort of console (I wish Microsoft would stop calling those "immediate window"...), and break-points we can disable or remove (no conditions on them, though).

That's all we need, really! The whole thing feels responsive and never froze my IE8. Honest!

B.6 Opera and Dragonfly

Opera takes an uncommon approach to providing developer tools. Its Drag-onfly tool is "both offline and online," because it is automatically downloaded and updated through the Internet when you open its pane in Opera. This means you need to be online the first time you use it, which should hardly be an issue. However, in my personal experience, I found it to kind of *require* being online to simply work. When offline, even if I had downloaded it before, it usually aborted launch because it was not able to connect to Opera's server (or something).

Its current version (alpha 3 at the time of this writing) clearly states it's still rough, and I can only hope the Opera folks will come to their senses, UI-wise, and rethink their gazillions-of-multilevel-tabs approach from the ground up. I would think all the other tools use a Firebug-like layout for a reason (it's simple enough yet powerful enough), but Opera goes on and builds this complex, intricate UI. It seems to have been getting better in recent versions, though.

For our purpose of debugging JavaScript, we just need what's in the Scripts tab, as displayed in Figure B.10, on the next page. You'll find toolbar but-tons for the usual stuff: run/resume, step over, step into, step out, and when to automatically trigger debug mode (for example, entering a function, encoun-tering an error). A drop-down list lets you display the source file (JavaScript or HTML) you want to debug through; the gutter next to the code lets you deal

Figure B.10: OPERA DRAGONFLY: SCRIPTS TAB

with breakpoints (right-click them to disable/reenable them); the Command line subtab under the code (yes, *under*...) provides a command line akin to the console; and righthand tabs provide access to the call stack and the local variables (in the *Inspection* tab).

In short, regular debugging can be done. I should confess, though, that my usual debugging cycle goes like this. First, code with either Safari or Firefox. Then verify and adjust (if needed) in "the other one" (either Firefox or Safari) and then in IE8, IE7, and IE6 (in that order). Finally, just to be sure, run a quick check in Opera and Chrome.

Thus, I follow the sequence I use for XHTML/CSS development. And just like markup and styling, once you get JavaScript working all right in Safari, Firefox, and the IE set, it usually works like a charm in Chrome and Opera. So, *debugging* in Opera is a rare need for me.

As a final note, know there is a Debug menu you can enable in Opera that gives you direct access to a number of functions reminiscent of Firefox's Web Developer Toolbar extension or Safari's Development menu. You can enable it by downloading a configuration file from within Opera.[6]

B.7 Virtual Machines Are Your Friends

Nowadays RAM is cheap. Most of use web developers code on machines with 4GB to 8GB of RAM, and the even more fortunate guys also run on

---

6. http://dragonfly.opera.com/app/debugmenu/DebugMenu.ini

SSD drives, making their overall experience *snappy*. On the heels of that phenomenon, virtual machines are getting a place of honor in any serious web developer's toolkit. VM software is cheap, even sometimes free, and options are quite numerous: Parallels Desktop[7] (on OS X, Windows, and Linux), VMware Fusion[8] (on OSX) or VMware Workstation[9] (on Windows), Sun's VirtualBox[10] (on just about any major OS), and many more still.

This commoditization of virtual machines lets us set up separate VMs to replicate all the browser situations we need to test for: IE6 to IE9, various versions of Safari, Chrome, Firefox, Opera, and so on. Most browsers will not let you run multiple versions of them on a single OS, or if they do, you will not get 100 percent identical behavior with that of said browser being the only version installed (case in point: the third-party MultipleIE package on Windows XP). VMs let you isolate successive versions in distinct OS images. Best of all, they let you run all this *on a single computer*. Typically, the host OS of choice is OS X; this is because of many factors, but the most relevant one to me is this: it's easy to set up a Linux or Windows in a VM, but it's very hard to run OS X inside a VM hosted on a non-Mac platform.

So by all means, go VM! This is so much more convenient than having to use multiple boxes or remote desktops where you keep colliding with other web developers using them at the same time.

B.8 The Network May Be Your Enemy

Sometimes you run into bugs that feel like *heisenbugs*:[11] they happen only when you *don't look*. As soon as you start stepping through your code or try to reproduce this on your development box, the elusive behavior is nowhere to be found. What gives?

This typically happens with Ajaxy stuff and high-latency or flaky connections (such as dial-ups or your corporate proxy barely keeping its head above water). To reproduce this kind of situation, you can use software known as *slow proxies*. My favorite tool in this area, and perhaps the most well-known, is Charles,[12] a Java-based tool (hence running on all major platforms). Not only does it let you throttle your perceived bandwidth, adjust your latency, and generally tweak your perceived network behavior, but it can also *record and replay* network sessions, and it provides detailed HTTP/HTTPS monitoring. Such tools are a godsend!

---

7. http://www.parallels.com/products/desktop/
8. http://www.vmware.com/fr/products/fusion/
9. http://www.vmware.com/products/workstation/
10. http://www.virtualbox.org/
11. http://en.wikipedia.org/wiki/Heisenbug
12. http://www.charlesproxy.com/

JavaScript Frameworks

JavaScript is a great language all by itself. But when it comes to interacting with its environment—such as the DOM, CSS, or XMLHttpRequest, to name only the most common client-side examples—going pure-JavaScript feels like building a skyscraper with a couple flintstone axes and a bunch of slippery logs. This is mostly because of two factors: the raw DOM interfaces have no reasonably high-level features, and most browsers deviate from web standards in their own oh-so-particular ways.

Because of this, a large number of JavaScript frameworks arose. Some of them gained enough traction and followers to become very well established, and I'll take you through the most prominent ones in this appendix.

Understand this right now: you *should very much* use a framework, perhaps even multiple frameworks, depending on the project or task at hand. The source code for such frameworks is very likely more robust, better tested, better documented, and better supported than what you would write on your own. Also, it's there already, so it can save you countless hours of frustrating development. Be pragmatic about it!

Choosing a framework is an important task, and you should pay attention to a number of factors. Here's a list you can use:

- How long has it been around? Is the code mature and stable? Is it well tested? (That is, is there a strong test suite maintained for it?)

- Is there a strong, lively community around it? Can I find help easily?

- Is there good documentation, preferably official?

- Does its API design work with my own sense of aesthetics? When I use this framework, do I end up with code I like to read and write?

- Does the framework serve a particular set of goals? Is it targeted at a specific developer audience? If so, do my goals, or my profile, fit?

On the other hand, here's an often-touted criterion you *should not care about*: *codebase size*. Gone are the days when serving JavaScript had to be slow, my friend. Nowadays, there are numerous techniques we can use to serve an otherwise large and well-commented codebase with lightning speed. These include comment stripping, code compression,[1] good HTTP response headers to help browsers cache, CDN distribution, and more.

Popular frameworks resort to most or all of these tools to ensure your pages will grab them in no time at all, so don't start arguing about a few measly source code kilobytes, OK?

C.1 Prototype, script.aculo.us, and Scripty2

Prototype is the first well-known JavaScript framework. Sam Stephenson created it at 37signals all the way back in February 2005 to provide a unified, easy-to-use API for DOM manipulation, event handling, and Ajax. Thomas Fuchs created script.aculo.us in 2005 as a companion API to Prototype, growing from the well-known Yellow Fade Technique to a full-blown suite for visual effects, drag-and-drop, and a few bare-bones UI widgets. Scripty2 is a complete rewrite and expansion of script.aculo.us, currently in beta, that's very much geared toward visual effects.

The team behind Prototype fluctuates around a kernel of about half a dozen volunteers, most prominently Sam, Tobie Langel, and Andrew Dupont. Available under an MIT license (basically, it's open source and usable anywhere), the complete source is available on GitHub for browsing, forking, and tweaking, and there's a feedback mailing list plus a bug report system.

An ecosystem has evolved around Prototype, including PDoc (a code inline documentation system), Evidence (a unit testing framework), Sprockets (an advanced JavaScript processing and concatenation tool), and Scripteka (a plug-ins repository). The community is alive and kicking, mostly on Google Groups. A number of books exist; to date, the most current are *Practical Prototype and script.aculo.us* [Dup08], by Andrew Dupont, and *Prototype and script.aculo.us* [Por07], by yours truly.

Although Prototype is generally considered the first well-known JavaScript framework, in the past two years its popularity has slowly been declining, apparently moving toward jQuery. I believe, however, that these two frameworks address distinct—although overlapping—sets of needs (and they certainly have very different code aesthetics).

Prototype's architecture, code aesthetics, and cohesive API design are very well suited to significant codebases with robust APIs, and its "porting" of many of Ruby's goodies (such as the Enumerable module) make a lot of algorithm-heavy code easy to write. It's a framework for people who want to embrace JavaScript and write awesome stuff with it, growing and maintaining

---

1. Avoid code *obfuscation*, though, or whoever debugs on top of it will hate you.

an application's codebase over time. So, it's probably not the best choice for people just trying to pull some feature off or cobble together a website using widgets and plug-ins without knowing much about the language.

Here's a quick recap of the current versions at the time of this writing and the URLs you're likely to need:

- Prototype is at http://prototypejs.org/; its current version is 1.7.

- script.aculo.us is at http://script.aculo.us/ (duh!); its current version is 1.8.3, and development is basically frozen, because focus shifted to Scripty2.

- Scripty2 can be found at http://scripty2.com/. It is currently in Alpha release 6.

- PDoc is at http://pdoc.org/.

- Sprockets is at http://getsprockets.org/.

- Scripteka is at http://scripteka.com/.

- The support mailing list is found at http://groups.google.com/group/ prototype-scriptaculous. You can also try the *#prototype* IRC channel on Freenode.

- The feedback mailing list is found at http://groups.google.com/group/ prototype-core. Do not ask for help there—use the support list!

- The official repository is on GitHub: http://github.com/sstephenson/ prototype.

- If you have bugs to report, first read the guide at http://prototypejs. org/contribute, prepare your report with care, and then head over to https://prototype.lighthouseapp.com/.

C.2   jQuery and jQuery UI

jQuery originated in August 2005 when John Resig, having played with Prototype, decided that although he loved the features, the API, and the general feel of the code, it didn't quite suit his own taste. So, he went and tried something different. John is a friendly JavaScript guru working at Mozilla, so his undertaking the development of a framework was, you could say, in the natural order of things. After a version 1.0 release in June 2006, jQuery has enjoyed a rapid uptake in the last two years, thanks to massive community-driving work. The jQuery project was formally founded in September 2009, and its version 1.4 was released in January 2010 amid a two-week online celebration and coding fest. (The current version at the time of this writing is 1.4.2.)

jQuery's focus is mostly on lowering the perceived barrier-to-entry for people wanting to spruce up their web pages with a bit of JavaScript without prior knowledge of the language (or sometimes of programming in general). Its API provides a lot of quick shortcuts targeted at the most common use cases, and a number of plug-ins (some of them grouped in the jQuery UI project) take care of the rest. Recently I've been hearing people describe jQuery as "a DSL for DOM manipulation" or state that "jQuery comes from selectors to code, allowing people who know CSS to use JavaScript." Although not entirely accurate (as in, a bit reductionist), such characterizations do capture the essence of jQuery.

The major driving force behind jQuery is its astounding team. Aside from almost two dozen people working on plug-ins projects, the core, the UI, and the website, its force very much lies with the half-dozen people who nurture the jQuery community through conferences, events, meetups, and the like. Having a number of corporate sponsors doesn't hurt, but the project itself remains open source, using a dual GPL/MIT license, hosted at GitHub, and allowing bug reports through Trac.

Around the core jQuery project and the jQuery UI, you'll find a number of magazines and conferences, meetups, user groups, and online forums. Several jQuery books have been published, including *jQuery for Dummies* [Bei10],[2] *jQuery in Action* [BK10], *jQuery: Novice to Ninja* [CS10], and *jQuery Cookbook* [Lin09].

As I mentioned, I believe jQuery and Prototype address somewhat different need sets. I cannot deny the many merits of jQuery, and I certainly see how appealing it is to large categories of users, such as those needing JavaScript as a mere tool toward quick ends, who don't want to have to learn too much API to get common tasks done in a snap. The teeming life of the jQuery community is also a big plus, because it inspires confidence in the project's longevity and level of support. jQuery is, at the time of this writing, at version 1.4.2.

Here's a list of the URLs you're likely to need or want to check out:

- The official website is http://jquery.com/.

- The official website for jQuery UI is http://jqueryui.com/.

- Source code is hosted at GitHub: http://github.com/jquery/jquery.

- Bug tracking can be found at http://dev.jquery.com/.

- All official forums can be found at http://docs.jquery.com/Discussion.

---

2. This goes to show how widely known the framework has become!

C.3 MooTools

Created in 2006 by Valerio Proietti, MooTools is like a handpicked subset of features—it's most of Prototype plus visual effects plus a few domain-specific tools (cookie management, SWFObject wrapper for Flash loading, and so on). Its original goals are to provide traditional, class-based object-programming features and to remain compact (admittedly, in this age of Google Ajax APIs, script concatenation, and gzipping, this latter aspect is a less effective selling point).

The project is split into MooTools Core (the framework itself) and MooTools More (the plug-in repository).

Supported by a core team of thirteen, MooTools is an open source, MIT-licensed project currently in version 1.2.4. It is hosted on GitHub, with bug tracking and feature requests on Lighthouse and support through a Google Group and a dedicated forum.

The significant book on MooTools is *MooTools Essentials* [New08].

It seems as if MooTools has, at least so far, the lowest popularity/reach among the frameworks in this appendix. Still, it does have a non-negligible developer mind share.

Here are a few pointers you may need:

- MooTools' official website is at http://mootools.net/.
- The source code is at http://github.com/mootools/mootools-core.
- Bug tracking and feature requests can be found at https://mootools.lighthouseapp.com/.
- You can get support and news on the Google Group at http://groups.google.com/group/mootools-users and the forum at http://mooforum.net/. There are also a number of docs and tutorials to get you up to speed on http://mootorial.com/.

C.4 YUI

The Yahoo! User Interface library, commonly dubbed YUI (which, as far as I know, is pronounced by spelling it), is part of a larger set of developer resources maintained by the Yahoo! Developer Network (YDN). The project started in 2005 and had its first release in early 2006. It is a very strong, modular, powerful framework, with perhaps a somewhat steep initial learning curve. Its core JavaScript functionality lies in "YUI 3," and there are numerous extra features, not necessarily JavaScript-related, in other modules. YUI is used intensively on Yahoo! "properties" (websites and online services

Yahoo! owns), so it certainly has a proven track record of stability and performance.

You should know that the convention for initializing the framework and accessing its modules and features changed drastically between versions 2 and 3, so be wary of old documentation and tutorials. Any calls starting with YAHOO. are basically version 2. Note, however, that since YUI 3.1 you can integrate older-style solutions and code more simply.

Although contribution to the core of YUI is not quite open source (despite a BSD license, actual contribution to this part of the codebase seems restricted to YDN), the YUI Gallery lets people contribute modules. You can also contribute bug reports and feature requests.

Most of the quality documentation about YUI is online, either at the official website for the framework or on the YUI Library website, which is very community-oriented. You'll also find a treasure trove of articles by Christian Heilmann, an evangelist at YDN, sprinkled across a number of popular web development online magazines. The docs contain hundreds of examples with step-by-step instructions. The quality of the docs perhaps explains why, at this point, there are precious few books about YUI, though. The only book I found of some significance dates back to YUI2: *Learning the Yahoo! User Interface Library* [Wel08].

YUI is fairly popular. However, YUI is mostly used in the rich Internet application (RIA) space, like Dojo, because it is perceived to be rather overkill (and overweight) for less-UI-intensive use cases. In that respect, it's often used in conjunction with other useful YDN resources such as the "reset" and "grid" style sheets. The community interaction is centralized at the official YUI Library website.

YUI sports a few very good "selling points":

- It has a very cohesive API (its style is consistent throughout).

- It's extremely well-tested and well-documented.

- It pays special attention to accessibility (for example, ARIA support).

- Its modular, load-on-demand approach, coupled with its massive CDN, keeps it very usable even in lightweight environments.

- It is officially maintained and supported by a large corporation (Yahoo!), which makes it a fairly low-risk bet when building your project's technology stack.

I do believe that you should favor a lighter-weight library for anything where that's sufficient, though. It makes for less stuff to absorb and digest. It also makes it easier for you to contribute quickly by fixing or extending stuff you need.

These are four URLs you should know:

- The official website is at http://developer.yahoo.com/yui/3/.

- The source code repository is at http://github.com/yui.

- Bug reports and feedback are found at http://yuilibrary.com/projects/yui3/report.

- Community resources in general are at http://yuilibrary.com/.

C.5 ExtJS

ExtJS is a full-blown RIA framework focusing on rich, desktop-like UI widgets such as tree views, datagrids, and dialog boxes. It started out in 2006 (I think) as an add-on by Jack Slocum, which you could use over Prototype, jQuery, or YUI. Since then, it has evolved into a stand-alone, large framework targeted specifically at building rich, desktop-style user interfaces; for instance, having nailed great datagrid, tree, and Ajax features early on, ExtJS is a popular tool for building website administration pages.

ExtJS is a product of the eponymous company, which provides related tools such as Ext Designer and the Ext GWT bridge. It is available under a triple license: GPLv3, commercial, and OEM. This license split caused quite a stir when it launched, not least because it essentially prevented use in non-GPL-compatible open source projects. On the other hand, it means you can get commercial tech support, training, and subscriptions from the library creators. It's too bad the repository is closed, accessible only through release snapshots on a custom download page. I couldn't find a prominent bug-tracking system, either, so all in all, despite a GPLv3 option, the project source doesn't look that open.

Like all good projects with a full-time, corporate workforce behind them,[3] ExtJS is moving apace. At the time of this writing, it's at version 3.1.1, and 2010 is expected to see several major releases leading up to 4.0.

Documentation is rather good, with an easily browsable—if sometimes terse —API reference, obviously built with ExtJS, and numerous complete, useful application samples. You'll also find a few books, most notably *ExtJS 3.0 Cookbook* [Ram09], released in late 2009, and *ExtJS in Action* [Gar10], due in summer 2010.

---

3. ExtJS has a six-person *management* team and a full-time developer team of unknown size.

Finally, given the somewhat proprietary nature of the project, the ecosystem is mostly limited to the official website, sporting forums and a good wiki-based Learning Center offering demos, screencasts, tutorials, and more.

These are the mandatory links:

- This is the ExtJS official website: http://extjs.com/.

- Download it at http://www.extjs.com/products/extjs/download.php.

- You can find the forum at http://www.extjs.com/forum/.

- The Learning Center's home is at http://www.extjs.com/learn/Main_Page.

C.6 Dojo

We will complete this tour of the most popular frameworks with Dojo. It was created in 2004 through the arduous and joint efforts of Alex Russell, Dylan Schiemann, and David Schontzler while at Informatica, and it released in big one-oh on November 5, 2007, getting split into Dojo (the core), Dijit (the UI widgets), and DojoX (the plug-ins and extended features).

Dojo plays in much the same space as ExtJS now. It's a major RIA framework with huge corporate backing. It is now nurtured by the Dojo Foundation, which includes corporate sponsors such as IBM, Google, AOL, Thomson Reuters, TIBCO, Zend, and Sitepen, to name only a few. Its current release at the time of this writing is 1.5.0. Unlike ExtJS though, Dojo is *actually* open source, being dual-licensed under the Academic Free License 2.1 and the new BSD license, and maintaining public GitHub, Subversion, and Bazaar repositories and an online bug tracking system.

Dojo is also close to projects that are now also under the umbrella of the Dojo Foundation, the most well-known ones being cometD and DWR, two early—and still relevant—systems for doing push notifications from the server to the browser (not to forget Sizzle, Persevere, and General Interface).

Dojo is very active at web development conferences (with T-shirts, subconferences, meetups, the works!) and in general maintains a lively community with dedicated forums. As far as community strength goes, it's probably second only to jQuery. You'll find a number of good books, too, including *Mastering Dojo* [RGR08], *Dojo: the Definitive Guide* [Rus08], *Practical Dojo Projects* [Zam08], and more recently *Getting StartED with Dojo* [Hay10].

The online docs are very good, split among a Quick Start Guide, a Reference Guide, and the API documentation, plus a cross point of entry using "popular solutions" that are task-oriented (for example, "Create charts from datasets").

In my opinion, should you need to create RIA-type, desktop-like applications based on web standards, Dojo should be your primary choice.

We'll wrap up this appendix with a quick list of Dojo's important URLs:

- This is the official website: http://www.dojotoolkit.org/.

- You can access the repository at http://svn.dojotoolkit.org/src/ (pity they don't use Git).

- You can find bug tracking and reporting at http://bugs.dojotoolkit.org/.

- You can engage with the community at http://www.dojotoolkit.org/community/.

Getting Help

Well, I certainly hope you found this book useful. Still, you'll need to find some solutions yourself, or you may need someone to confirm you're on track. So, where can you get more help and engage with other people about all this?

D.1 Help on JavaScript in General

Having great frameworks around is no excuse for not knowing your Java-Script. Sometimes you actually need to dive in and write some actual code, or perhaps you can't make use of your usual framework for various reasons (performance on mobile devices,[1] anyone?).

Newsgroups

Remember the time before DSL was (almost) everywhere? Before Google Groups? Before Google, actually? Well, perhaps you weren't developing back then, but we had *Usenet*. It's still around, and recently, a new generation has discovered how good it can be at, say, sharing binary files. Better still, it has *newsgroups* for every programming language known to man.

Every ISP provides newsgroup access; it's that weird "NNTP server" thing you saw on your subscription papers. And most aggregators, feed readers, and even email clients—Thunderbird, Entourage, Outlook, and, yes, even Outlook Express—let you connect to an NNTP server and subscribe to newsgroups of your choice. (Depending on your ISP, you'll have your pick of thousands.)

Heck, even if you don't want to access these groups that way, Google Groups maintains bridges to most useful newsgroups, including the following ones:

- The core of all the action is at comp.lang.javascript. (The address is short for *COMPuter LANGuage JavaScript*.) It's been around for ages and remains *the* main location for all online discussions related

---

1. Except if you're using the awesome, just-released zepto.js library by Thomas Fuchs: http://github.com/madrobby/zepto. Or even go fastest-ever with vapor.js: http://github.com/madrobby/vapor.js.

to the language itself. You'll find all kinds of attendees, from complete newbies to awesome gurus.

- You can also get non-English discussion in the few language-specific subgroups, like de.comp.lang.javascript, fr.comp.lang.javascript, japan.comp.lang.javascript, and the like.

Mailing Lists and Forums

You'll find plenty of forums out there, with quality varying from abysmal to awesome, depending on who's posting. Just stay away from cut-and-paste dumpsters; this is how bad practices keep popping up everywhere.

- Google Groups maintains a bridge on the newsgroups I mentioned before, so you could head there.[2]

- Sitepoint is usually pretty good, so you could try their JavaScript forum.[3]

- Webdeveloper has a lot of activity.[4]

But seriously, go with the first one (the newsgroup bridge) whenever possible. There's a higher signal-to-noise ratio.

IRC Channels

Ah, IRC. This is another old-timer, but it's great because, well, it's *instant messaging*. On the other hand, its usefulness depends on whether knowledgeable people are logged in at the same time you are.

The main channel, on irc.freenode.net, is ##javascript. It usually boasts between 300 and 400 attendees at any given time. With a bit of poking around, you can also find a few good non-English channels.

Further Reading

You can find a number of authoritative books on JavaScript. I've listed many in the bibliography, but I'll comment on a few here:

- *JavaScript: The Definitive Guide* [Fla06], by David Flanagan, is widely acknowledged as *the* JavaScript bible, which is funny since the *JavaScript Bible* [Goo07] is by Danny Goodman, prefaced by Brendan Eich. (A seventh edition is due very soon.)

- You'll also want to take a look at *JavaScript: The Good Parts* [Cro08], by Douglas Crockford, the guy behind JSON and JSLint, who keeps telling us not to use two-thirds of what the language offers (grin).

---

2.   http://groups.google.com/group/comp.lang.javascript
3.   http://www.sitepoint.com/forums/forumdisplay.php?f=15
4.   http://www.webdeveloper.com/forum/forumdisplay.php?forumid=3

- John Resig, of jQuery fame, recently wrote what seems to be a great little book at Sitepoint: *Secrets of the JavaScript Ninja* [Res09].

- Still at Sitepoint, although slightly more dated, is a great book by several authors: *The Art and Science of JavaScript* [AEH⁺07].

- Evangelist extraordinaire Chris Heilmann authored *Beginning JavaScript with DOM Scripting and Ajax: From Novice to Professional* [Hei06], which is also a great read.

- I would be remiss if I did not add Thomas Fuchs and Amy Hoy's latest jewel, which is really a companion tool for performance, performance, and performance: *JavaScript Performance Rocks!* [HF09].

D.2 Help on Frameworks

This section brings together the various online resources sprinkled through Appendix C.

Prototype and script.aculo.us

- Official support list[5]
- Online API docs[6]
- IRC channels: #prototype and #scriptaculous on Freenode

Books:

- *Practical Prototype and script.aculo.us* [Dup08], by Andrew Dupont
- *Prototype and script.aculo.us* [Por07], by yours truly

jQuery

- Official forums[7]
- Tutorials[8]
- API documentation[9]
- IRC channel: #jquery on Freenode

Books:

- *jQuery for Dummies* [Bei10] by Lynn Beighley
- *jQuery in Action* [BK10] by Bear Bibault and Yehuda Kata (and originally John Resig)
- *jQuery: Novice to Ninja* [CS10] by Earle Castledine and Craig Sharkie

---

5. http://groups.google.com/group/prototype-scriptaculous
6. http://api.prototypejs.org/ and http://wiki.github.com/madrobby/scriptaculous/
7. http://forum.jquery.com/
8. http://docs.jquery.com/Tutorials
9. http://docs.jquery.com/Main_Page

- *jQuery Cookbook* [Lin09] by Cody Lindley

MooTools

- Official support list[10]
- Forum[11]
- Tutorials[12]
- API documentation[13]

Books:

- *MooTools Essentials* [New08] by Aaron Newton

YUI

- Forum[14]
- Documentation[15]
- IRC channel: #yui on Freenode (not very active, though)

Books:

- *Learning the Yahoo! User Interface library* [Wel08], by Dan Wellman

ExtJS

- Forum[16]
- Demos[17]
- API documentation[18]
- Learning Center[19]
- IRC channels: #extjs on Freenode (not very active though)

Books:

- *ExtJS 3.0 Cookbook* [Ram09], by Jorge Ramon
- *ExtJS in Action* [Gar10], by Jesus Garcia

---

10. http://groups.google.com/group/mootools-users
11. http://mooforum.net/
12. http://mootorial.com/
13. http://mootools.net/docs/core
14. http://yuilibrary.com/forum/
15. http://developer.yahoo.com/yui/3/
16. http://www.extjs.com/forum/
17. http://www.extjs.com/deploy/dev/examples/
18. http://www.extjs.com/deploy/dev/docs/
19. http://www.extjs.com/learn/Main_Page

Dojo

- Forum[20]
- API documentation and tutorials[21]
- IRC channels: #dojo on Freenode

Books:

- *Mastering Dojo* [RGR08], by Craig Riecke, Rawld Gill, and Alex Russell
- *Dojo: the Definitive Guide* [Rus08], by Matthew A. Russell
- *Practical Dojo Projects* [Zam08], by Frank Zammetti

---

20. http://www.dojotoolkit.org/community/
21. http://www.dojotoolkit.org/documentation/

Bibliography

[AEH+07]   Cameron Adams, James Edwards, Christian Heilmann, Michael Mahemoff, Ara Pehlivanian, Dan Webb, and Simon Willison. *The Art and Science of JavaScript*. Sitepoint, 2007.

[Bei10]   Lynn Beighley. *jQuery for Dummies*. For Dummies, 2010.

[BK10]   Bear Bibeault and Yehuda Katz. *jQuery in Action*. Manning Publications Co., Greenwich, CT, second edition, 2010.

[Cro08]   Douglas Crockford. *JavaScript: The Good Parts*. O'Reilly Media, Inc. / Yahoo! Press, Sebastopol, CA, 2008.

[CS10]   Earle Castledine and Craig Sharkie. *jQuery: Novice to Ninja*. Sitepoint, San Francisco, CA, 2010.

[Dup08]   Andrew Dupont. *Practical Prototype and script.aculo.us*. Apress, New York, NY, 2008.

[Fla06]   David Flanagan. *JavaScript: The Definitive Guide*. O'Reilly Media, Inc., Sebastopol, CA, fifth edition, 2006.

[Gar10]   Jesus Garcia. *ExtJS in Action*. Manning Publications Co., Greenwich, CT, 2010.

[Goo07]   Danny Goodman. *JavaScript Bible*. John Wiley & Sons, 2007.

[Hay10]   Kyle Hayes. *Getting StartED with Dojo*. Friends of ED, New York, NY, 2010.

[Hei06]   Christian Heilmann. *Beginning JavaScript with DOM Scripting and Ajax: From Novice to Professional*. Apress, New York, NY, 2006.

[HF09]   Amy Hoy and Thomas Fuchs. *JavaScript Performance Rocks!* Slash7, Vienna, Austria, 2009.

[Lin09]   Cody Lindley. *jQuery Cookbook*. O'Reilly Media, Inc., Sebastopol, CA, 2009.

[New08]   Aaron Newton. *MooTools Essentials*. Apress, 2008.

[Por07]   Christophe Porteneuve. *Prototype and script.aculo.us: You never knew JavaScript could do this!* The Pragmatic Programmers, LLC, Raleigh, NC, and Dallas, TX, 2007.

[Ram09]   Jorge Ramon. *ExtJS 3.0 Cookbook*. Packt, Birmingham, UK, 2009.

[Res09]   John Resig. *Secrets of the JavaScript Ninja*. Manning Publications Co., Greenwich, CT, 2009.

[RGR08]   Craig Riecke, Rawld Gill, and Alex Russell. *Mastering Dojo: JavaScript and Ajax Tools for Great Web Experiences*. The Pragmatic Programmers, LLC, Raleigh, NC, and Dallas, TX, 2008.

[Rus08]   Matthew A. Russell. *Dojo: the Definitive Guide*. O'Reilly Media, Inc., Sebastopol, CA, 2008.

[Wel08]   Dan Wellman. *Learning the Yahoo! User Interface library*. Packt, Birmingham, UK, 2008.

[Zam08]   Frank Zammetti. *Practical Dojo Projects*. Apress, New York, NY, 2008.

Index

The Pragmatic Bookshelf

Available in paperback and DRM-free eBooks, our titles are here to help you stay on top of your game. The following are in print as of October 2010; be sure to check our website at pragprog.com for newer titles.

Title	Year	ISBN	Pages
	2008	9780978739225	464
Advanced Rails Recipes: 84 New Ways to Build Stunning Rails Apps			
Agile Coaching	2009	9781934356432	248
Agile Retrospectives: Making Good Teams Great	2006	9780977616640	200
Agile Web Development with Rails	2009	9781934356166	792
Beginning Mac Programming: Develop with Objective-C and Cocoa	2010	9781934356517	300
Behind Closed Doors: Secrets of Great Management	2005	9780976694021	192
Best of Ruby Quiz	2006	9780976694076	304
Cocoa Programming: A Quick-Start Guide for Developers	2010	9781934356302	450
Core Animation for Mac OS X and the iPhone: Creating Compelling Dynamic User Interfaces	2008	9781934356104	200
Core Data: Apple's API for Persisting Data on Mac OS X	2009	9781934356326	256
Data Crunching: Solve Everyday Problems using Java, Python, and More	2005	9780974514079	208
Debug It! Find, Repair, and Prevent Bugs in Your Code	2009	9781934356289	232
Deploying Rails Applications: A Step-by-Step Guide	2008	9780978739201	280
Design Accessible Web Sites: 36 Keys to Creating Content for All Audiences and Platforms	2007	9781934356029	336
Desktop GIS: Mapping the Planet with Open Source Tools	2008	9781934356067	368
Domain-Driven Design Using Naked Objects	2009	9781934356449	375
Enterprise Integration with Ruby	2006	9780976694069	360
Enterprise Recipes with Ruby and Rails	2008	9781934356234	416
Everyday Scripting with Ruby: for Teams, Testers, and You	2007	9780977616619	320
ExpressionEngine 2: A Quick-Start Guide	2010	9781934356524	250
From Java To Ruby: Things Every Manager Should Know	2006	9780976694090	160
FXRuby: Create Lean and Mean GUIs with Ruby	2008	9781934356074	240
GIS for Web Developers: Adding Where to Your Web Applications	2007	9780974514093	275
Google Maps API: Adding Where to Your Applications	2006	PDF-Only	83
Grails: A Quick-Start Guide	2009	9781934356463	200
Groovy Recipes: Greasing the Wheels of Java	2008	9780978739294	264
Hello, Android: Introducing Google's Mobile Development Platform	2010	9781934356562	320

Continued on next page

Title	Year	ISBN	Pages
Interface Oriented Design	2006	9780976694052	240
iPad Programming: A Quick-Start Guide for iPhone Developers	2010	9781934356579	248
iPhone SDK Development	2009	9781934356258	576
Land the Tech Job You Love	2009	9781934356265	280
Language Implementation Patterns: Create Your Own Domain-Specific and General Programming Languages	2009	9781934356456	350
Learn to Program	2009	9781934356364	240
Manage It! Your Guide to Modern Pragmatic Project Management	2007	9780978739249	360
Manage Your Project Portfolio: Increase Your Capacity and Finish More Projects	2009	9781934356296	200
Mastering Dojo: JavaScript and Ajax Tools for Great Web Experiences	2008	9781934356111	568
Metaprogramming Ruby: Program Like the Ruby Pros	2010	9781934356470	240
Modular Java: Creating Flexible Applications with OSGi and Spring	2009	9781934356401	260
No Fluff Just Stuff 2006 Anthology	2006	9780977616664	240
No Fluff Just Stuff 2007 Anthology	2007	9780978739287	320
Pomodoro Technique Illustrated: The Easy Way to Do More in Less Time	2009	9781934356500	144
Practical Programming: An Introduction to Computer Science Using Python	2009	9781934356272	350
Practices of an Agile Developer	2006	9780974514086	208
Pragmatic Guide to Git	2010	9781934356722	168
Pragmatic Project Automation: How to Build, Deploy, and Monitor Java Applications	2004	9780974514031	176
Pragmatic Thinking and Learning: Refactor Your Wetware	2008	9781934356050	288
Pragmatic Unit Testing in C# with NUnit	2007	9780977616671	176
Pragmatic Unit Testing in Java with JUnit	2003	9780974514017	160
Pragmatic Version Control using CVS	2003	9780974514000	176
Pragmatic Version Control Using Git	2008	9781934356159	200
Pragmatic Version Control using Subversion	2006	9780977616657	248
Programming Clojure	2009	9781934356333	304
Programming Cocoa with Ruby: Create Compelling Mac Apps Using RubyCocoa	2009	9781934356197	300
Programming Erlang: Software for a Concurrent World	2007	9781934356005	536
Programming Groovy: Dynamic Productivity for the Java Developer	2008	9781934356098	320
Programming Ruby: The Pragmatic Programmers' Guide	2004	9780974514055	864
Programming Ruby 1.9: The Pragmatic Programmers' Guide	2009	9781934356081	960

Continued on next page

Title	Year	ISBN	Pages
Programming Scala: Tackle Multi-Core Complexity on the Java Virtual Machine	2009	9781934356319	250
Prototype and script.aculo.us: You Never Knew JavaScript Could Do This!	2007	9781934356012	448
Rails for .NET Developers	2008	9781934356203	300
Rails for Java Developers	2007	9780977616695	336
Rails for PHP Developers	2008	9781934356043	432
Rails Recipes	2006	9780977616602	350
Rapid GUI Development with QtRuby	2005	PDF-Only	83
Release It! Design and Deploy Production-Ready Software	2007	9780978739218	368
Scripted GUI Testing with Ruby	2008	9781934356180	192
Seven Languages in Seven Weeks: A Pragmatic Guide to Learning Programming Languages	2010	9781934356593	300
Ship It! A Practical Guide to Successful Software Projects	2005	9780974514048	224
SQL Antipatterns: Avoiding the Pitfalls of Database Programming	2010	9781934356555	352
Stripes ...and Java Web Development Is Fun Again	2008	9781934356210	375
Test-Drive ASP.NET MVC	2010	9781934356531	296
TextMate: Power Editing for the Mac	2007	9780978739232	208
The Agile Samurai: How Agile Masters Deliver Great Software	2010	9781934356586	280
The Definitive ANTLR Reference: Building Domain-Specific Languages	2007	9780978739256	384
The Passionate Programmer: Creating a Remarkable Career in Software Development	2009	9781934356340	200
ThoughtWorks Anthology	2008	9781934356142	240
Ubuntu Kung Fu: Tips, Tricks, Hints, and Hacks	2008	9781934356227	400
Web Design for Developers: A Programmer's Guide to Design Tools and Techniques	2009	9781934356135	300

More Fun With Languages

Seven Languages in Seven Weeks

In this book you'll get a hands-on tour of Clojure, Haskell, Io, Prolog, Scala, Erlang, and Ruby. Whether or not your favorite language is on that list, you'll broaden your perspective of programming by examining these languages side-by-side. You'll learn something new from each, and best of all, you'll learn how to learn a language quickly.

Seven Languages in Seven Weeks: A Pragmatic Guide to Learning Programming Languages
Bruce A. Tate
(300 pages) ISBN: 978-1934356-59-3. $34.95
http://pragprog.com/titles/btlang

Seven Languages
in Seven Weeks

A Pragmatic
Guide to
Learning
Programming
Languages

Bruce A. Tate
Edited by Jacquelyn Carter

Language Implementation Patterns

Learn to build configuration file readers, data readers, model-driven code generators, source-to-source translators, source analyzers, and interpreters. You don't need a background in computer science—ANTLR creator Terence Parr demystifies language implementation by breaking it down into the most common design patterns. Pattern by pattern, you'll learn the key skills you need to implement your own computer languages.

Language Implementation Patterns: Create Your Own Domain-Specific and General Programming Languages
Terence Parr
(350 pages) ISBN: 978-1934356-45-6. $34.95
http://pragprog.com/titles/tpdsl

Language
Implementation
Patterns

Create Your Own Domain-
Specific and General
Programming Languages

Terence Parr

The Pragmatic Bookshelf

The Pragmatic Bookshelf features books written by developers for developers. The titles continue the well-known Pragmatic Programmer style and continue to garner awards and rave reviews. As development gets more and more difficult, the Pragmatic Programmers will be there with more titles and products to help you stay on top of your game.

Visit Us Online

Pragmatic Guide to JavaScript
http://pragprog.com/titles/pg_js
Source code from this book, errata, and other resources. Come give us feedback, too!

Register for Updates
http://pragprog.com/updates
Be notified when updates and new books become available.

Join the Community
http://pragprog.com/community
Read our weblogs, join our online discussions, participate in our mailing list, interact with our wiki, and benefit from the experience of other Pragmatic Programmers.

New and Noteworthy
http://pragprog.com/news
Check out the latest pragmatic developments, new titles and other offerings.

Save on the eBook

Save on the eBook versions of this title. Owning the paper version of this book entitles you to purchase the electronic versions at a terrific discount.

PDFs are great for carrying around on your laptop—they are hyperlinked, have color, and are fully searchable. Most titles are also available for the iPhone and iPod touch, Amazon Kindle, and other popular e-book readers.

Buy now at pragprog.com/coupon.

Contact Us

Online Orders:	www.pragprog.com/catalog
Customer Service:	support@pragprog.com
Non-English Versions:	translations@pragprog.com
Pragmatic Teaching:	academic@pragprog.com
Author Proposals:	proposals@pragprog.com
Contact us:	1-800-699-PROG (+1 919 847 3884)